BARRY SANDERS

emmis
books

BARRY SANDERS
Now You See Him...

ISBN 1-57860-139-8

Photos courtesy of:
Getty Images
Hulton Archive
AP Worldwide
NFL Photos
The Wichita Eagle
Oklahoma State University
Lauren Sanders and Slice of Life Photography
The Sanders Family

EDITED BY JACK HEFFRON
COVER AND INTERIOR DESIGNED BY STEPHEN SULLIVAN
COVER PHOTO BY: ALLEN KEE/NFL PHOTOS

CONTENTS

THANKS TO

Lauren, BJ, Nigel, Mom, Dad and the entire Sanders Family,
Mark E. McCormick, John Madden, all my teammates at Wichita North,
OSU, and in Detroit, Coach B, Coach Jones, Coach Fontes, Coach Ross, and
all the assistants coaches on their staffs, to those who wrote sidebars
for the book (Lomas Brown, Emmitt Smith, Mike Singletary, Wayne Fontes,
Louis Oliver, Kevin Glover) Jeff (JB) Bernstein and Eric Levin from Pro Access,
Richard Hunt, Jack Heffron, and Steve Sullivan from Emmis Books, Bo Rader
and *The Wichita Eagle*, NFL Films, the NFL Network, NFL Properties,
NFL Player's Inc., NFL Photos, the Detroit Lions, Oklahoma State University,
Wichita North High School, Mick Thompson, Dr. Harry Birdwell, Joe Muller,
Steve Buzzard, Tom Dirato, Bill Keenist, Steve Sabol, Jeanie Diblin,
John Collins, Dan Margolis, Traci Perlman, Gene Upshaw, Doug Allen,
Pat Allen, LaShun Lawson, Howard Skall, Jerry Borreson, Mike Pullwher,
David Ware, C. Lamont Smith, Peter Schaeffer, ESPN, CBS, FOX, ABC,
the College Football Hall of Fame, the NCAA Hall of Champions,
and the Pro Football Hall of Fame.

In loving memory of my sister Nancy.

INTRODUCTION
by John Madden

On the annual Thanksgiving Day game I used to give a "turkey leg" to the players who had a great game. Barry Sanders was one of those guys who you could give the leg as soon as the turkey was finished cooking. In every game he made moves that you'd never seen before, moves that made you say, "This can't be." He was the first guy I remember who could do what is now called a "jump cut," where the player jumps in the air and changes direction. When he started doing that move, we didn't even have a name for it.

During his career, players on other teams would talk about how hard he was to tackle. You didn't just miss a tackle, you got embarrassed. The defenders didn't like seeing themselves later on television or on a highlight reel looking silly. When you asked them about trying to tackle Barry Sanders, a lot of them would mention that.

Every person who was in the game at that time said, "Barry is the guy who I would pay to go see." Of course, that's a cliché used by people who never really pay to see games, but it's a way of saying that a player is special. It didn't matter where Detroit was in the standings or how meaningful the game was, if you had the chance to see Barry Sanders play, he was worth it. He was going to do things in every game he played that you had never seen anybody do before.

As his career developed, we came to appreciate that he was someone truly special. There are good running backs, and then there are some backs who play at a completely different level. Walter Payton was a great running back because he could do everything—run and catch the ball and block. Jim Brown was a great runner, but he was different, more of a big, bruising guy. O.J. Simpson had moves and speed. Emmitt Smith in his prime had everything. Barry was on that level too.

But he was more than a unique player on the field. He was unique off the field. And everyone who knew him felt that way. I've learned through the years that players can't help being jealous of other players. When you interview them, they'll rarely talk in glowing terms about another player. They'd rather talk about themselves. If they're going to say something nice about another player, they'll talk about a teammate. But I've never heard a single player say something negative about Barry. Guys from other teams would talk about him as if they were talking about a teammate. They mostly would talk about how classy he was.

He was the most unassuming superstar I've ever met. He mentioned to me once that he was taking college classes at Oakland University in the suburbs of Detroit during the season. He's a famous athlete, a local hero, and he's taking classes! I said, "How can you do that?" He said, "They don't know I'm there." I said, "How can they not know?" He said, "Because I don't tell them."

One of the things I enjoyed about Barry Sanders was the way he'd nonchalantly hand the ball to the official after a touchdown—as if it were no big deal. Most guys want to be noticed after a touchdown. They're doing their celebrations, dancing around or jumping into the stands. Barry became the exception. He got more notice for not celebrating. When he scored or did something amazing, that was sufficient. He didn't need to do anything else.

He was always very approachable—so cooperative, in fact, that it was tempting to take him for granted and ask him anything. I was talking to him one time about his new contract, and I said, "How much do you make?" He looked at me and said, "How much do you make?" I thought, okay, that's right. It's none of my business. But he was so unassuming you'd forget that.

I got to know him well during his career, and I also heard about him from other players who had Barry Sanders stories. Lomas Brown, for example, has started a second career telling Barry Sanders stories. And every married guy who played for the Lions had stories about Barry coming by for dinner and about how much he could eat. He was a little guy, but I guess he ate a lot. Then after dinner he'd lay on the floor with the kids and play with them, get them all worked up, and then he'd leave while the kids were still bouncing off the walls. The guys who played with him, his teammates, loved him.

To understand the true Barry Sanders, remember the way he left football. That was pure Barry. He played his last game without telling anyone. There were no parades, no big "Barry Sanders Day," nothing like that. When he was finished, he walked away. Everyone was upset with him because he did it his way; he didn't do it their way.

At the time, some people thought his retiring was a ploy to get a better contract. But knowing Barry, I knew it wasn't a ploy. He doesn't do things that way. At the same time, even though I had gotten to know him, I had no indication that he was planning to retire. I didn't see it coming. Some guys will talk about retiring before they do it. They'll let you know they're thinking about it, but not Barry. He wasn't a big talker. When he was finished, he was finished. It was frustrating for him, I think, to be such a great player and playing for a team that didn't win. A player like that wants to win a Super Bowl.

When you lose a superstar like Barry Sanders, it takes something out of the game for a while. His absence was particularly noticeable on Thanksgiving Day. Detroit was never all that good, but they had the tradition of playing on the holiday, and you could always count on Barry Sanders doing something miraculous. He became part of the tradition. On Thanksgiving Day, you knew you were going to get to see Barry Sanders play.

I picked him for a lot of the annual All-Madden teams, because he was my kind of player. If somebody asks what you want in a running back, you have to answer, "I want Barry Sanders." He was the whole package. You wouldn't take him only because he could break away for a touchdown on any play, even though he could do that. You would take him because he had all the ingredients. He was the guy you wanted on your side. He could do anything. And he got along with everyone. His teammates loved him. When kids in his neighborhood were choosing sides for a game, he was probably always picked first. He was probably never *it* in tag.

Barry was truly special in a lot of ways, and anybody who is a real football fan misses seeing Barry Sanders play.

NOW YOU SEE HIM

VOLUTSIA'S CALLING

I was born and raised in Wichita, Kansas, a city with a rich and interesting history, most of which I've learned from my friend Mark, who has a keen interest in the subject. A local historian tells the story of how in 1750, a group of French explorers, in search of gold, unwittingly founded the city. As the explorers navigated the Arkansas River (and that's pronounced R-Kansas) to its source at the foot of the Rocky Mountains, they came across a Spanish pack train loaded with gold. The French robbed the Spanish, filled the boats with gold, and headed back down the river.

When they approached an island where the Arkansas and Little Arkansas rivers meet, they made camp.

That night, they were attacked by Indians, and only one man escaped to tell the story. He never came back for the gold, but a later map showed the area now known as Wichita marked as a gold mine. And as people arrived in search of gold, Wichita was born.

Legendary lawman Bat Masterson called the area home. Wyatt Earp was fired by the City of Wichita after prostitution money he collected turned up missing. Billy the Kid witnessed numerous gunfights in the city, and his mother's signature is on the city's charter. By June of 1887, the city ranked third nationally in volume of real estate transactions behind only New York and Kansas City and ahead of Chicago and Philadelphia. Town leaders nicknamed Wichita "The Peerless Princess of the Prairie." Shortly after, an economic crisis crippled the town and rolled back the rapid expansion. People left almost as quickly as they'd come.

Grit and enterprise, however, saved the town. Walt Anderson, who founded White Castle hamburgers in the city, helped to usher in a tradition of entrepreneurship. The country's first Phillips 66 gas station opened in Wichita, and people such as Walter Beech and Clyde Cessna built an aircraft industry that marked the city as the "Air Capital of the World." Frank and Dan Carney borrowed six hundred dollars from their mother to found what would become the international restaurant icon Pizza Hut. Perhaps, as the historian says in her article, there may actually have been gold here.

I was born here—on July 16, 1968.

My childhood wasn't much different from the average American childhood. I had sisters who could work my last nerve. I had an older brother who used to hold me down and punch the air out of my chest. We threw rocks at each other, played basketball and tackle-

Our house at 2049 North Volutsia Avenue *(above)* was always full of kids—cousins, neighbors, and a lot of Sanders boys and girls *(previous page and page 9)*. In grade school *(right)*, I became obsessed with sports.

the-man-with-the-ball all day. We rode our bicycles in the summer, swam at the McAdams Park pool, and ate penny candy till our bellies swelled.

The two-block stretch of North Volutsia Avenue I grew up on, however, was special. It could have set the gold standard for achievement most anywhere in white or black America. Between my house at 2049 to the house at 1922, black parents raised a doctor now practicing in Kansas City, a federal agent

for the Internal Revenue Service, an airplane pilot, an *Ebony* fashion model, a preacher, a host of teachers and college graduates with advanced degrees, two journalists, at least three nurses, and one All-Pro running back.

These children were raised by parents who were teachers, pilots, a state representative, a construction company owner, nurses, and blue-collar laborers. They were all special people drawn to a special place.

KANSAS AND WICHITA IN BLACK HISTORY

After I turned pro, I often was asked by black people who learned I was from Wichita, "Are there blacks in Kansas?" Though I assured them there were many blacks, I was an adult before I realized the pivotal role Kansas played in black history. Again, my friend Mark told me a good many of these facts. Kansas entered the Union in 1861 as a free state, and its first years were troubled by violence as the national issue of slavery boiled into the start of the Civil War. Statehood did not come to Kansas without a significant cost in human life. Abolitionist John Brown led numerous raids and battles to maintain that status and helped earn the state the name "Bleeding Kansas."

The state has produced many distinguished black Americans. Filmmaker, author, and Pulitzer-prize-winning photographer Gordon Parks hails from Ft. Scott, Kansas. Langston Hughes, the poet laureate of Harlem, called Kansas home in his childhood, as did Gwendolyn Brooks, the first black woman to win a Pulitzer Prize in literature.

And so when I'm asked if there are black people in Kansas, the answer is "Yep," and none of the black folks anywhere in the country would have had any semblance of freedom if not for our people's history in my home state. When the U.S. Supreme Court took up the issue of school desegregation in 1954, in the now famous Brown vs. Board of Education case, Topeka found itself at the center of what would be a landmark decision to begin breaking down decades-old racial boundaries.

Many Wichitans believe the nation's first lunch counter sit-in took place in downtown Wichita in 1958. Members of an NAACP youth group started the protest at Dockum's drugstore downtown. Led by a young man named Ronald Walters, the students' campaign successfully opened the store's lunch counter to black citizens, who previously had to place orders at the back-door and eat in the alley. Walters would grow up to become one of the nation's foremost political scientists and intellectuals. He served as the Reverend Jesse Jackson's campaign manager in Jackson's 1984 bid for the presidency, directed the floor operations during the 1988 Democratic National Convention, and continues to offer political commentary on a variety of network and cable news programs, such as CNN's "Crossfire." Walters grew up on Madison Avenue, just a few blocks away from my childhood home on North Volutsia.

I spent hours shooting hoops and playing bumper pool in the recreation center designed by black Wichita blue-blood Charles McAfee. McAfee's family arrived with the city's earliest settlers, and his architectural works earned him a chapter in the book *Black Genius*. Though his buildings in Wichita and across the country have won numerous architectural awards, he's perhaps best known for the work done by the Atlanta arm of his firm, run by his daughter Cheryl, in designing all thirty-two Olympic venues for the 1996 Olympics in Atlanta.

McAfee grew up several blocks away from my childhood home in an area that served as the business and cultural center of town for black citizens in segregated

One of my first Biddy Basketball teams. That's me seated on the far left.

Wichita. During his childhood, that neighborhood produced a dozen African Americans with doctoral degrees, virtually all of whom had to leave the city in search of career opportunities elsewhere.

One Wichitan who left was Donald Hollowell, who may be best known in civil rights circles as the lawyer who helped free the Reverend Martin Luther King, Jr. from the brutal confines of Reidsville Prison in Georgia, where he was confined for a creative traffic violation charge. But he's also the man who gave Washington D.C. powerbroker Vernon Jordan his first job and was the courageous lawyer who defended black clients in front of all-white juries in dangerous, rural areas—and won.

The stubborn focus on education and achievement that drove these people surely influenced my parents' generation, who worked hard to make sure that the elevator to success didn't leave without their children.

SPORTS

It would be difficult to underestimate the importance of sports in my childhood. Daddy, a lifelong fan of the Kansas Jayhawk basketball team and Oklahoma Sooner football team, always seemed to have the chatter of a game on the television or on the radio. And in the barbershop, we'd listen to the heated arguments among the old men about the failings and fortunes of local and regional teams.

From the time my brother Byron and I were small, Daddy enrolled us in Biddy Basketball and Little League football. We had electric football sets and Oakland Raider winter coats and ski caps. Our lives as children revolved around sports. At school, after school, and on Saturdays, we'd gather in corner lots and sometimes crawl over the fence at Wichita State University's football stadium or line the walls of the basement in what is now the Lynette Woodard Recreation Center. We'd play pick-up basketball games at the center until Cliff Fanning, who ran the place, chased us off the court.

If we couldn't play basketball at the center, we'd rip the spokes out of a bicycle wheel and nail the rim to a tree for a hoop. For pick-up football games, we'd mark off a field on a duplex lawn and designate a tree as one end zone and a sidewalk as the other. On Friday nights in the fall, we'd pile into the back of Daddy's pick-up and watch high school football games and play tackle-the-man on the sidelines at halftime.

We regarded the older athletes around us—neighborhood stars from the court, track, or football field—with awe. We felt this way toward these guys because of the city's and the state's rich sports tradition. Local lore says the basketball fast break was created at Wichita East High School by legendary head coach Ralph

Miller, who later coached at the University of Iowa. East High also produced legendary miler Jim Ryun.

In 1988, the year I won the Heisman Trophy, the University of Kansas, led by forward Danny Manning and coach Larry Brown, won the NCAA championship. The next year, Wichita State University won the College World Series. Sports seemed to bring us together in a way nothing else could.

In our neighborhood, we were generally safe among the blocks and blocks of modest, lower-middle-class homes. Most families had children, and we all played football and basketball together in the parks and the lots dotting what was then called Northeast Wichita. But the streets did call out to a lot of people, and more than a few answered. We had friends lured by the siren call of life on street corners. The older we got, the wider the concentric circles of our lives began taking in people who lived on delinquency's edge. Most of us stayed out of trouble and laughed at friends who smoked weed and drank Canadian Mist. But as graduation approached and life paths beyond North High grew clouded, more and more of us made the leap from the curb into the street.

But Volutsia had another sort of calling, too.

The adults who raised us called on us to work hard and to stretch that work into some sort of future for ourselves. We also chose diverse career paths, as I said before. The differences in those paths indicates to me that we didn't simply select jobs or even careers. We followed a calling, a choice of life's work that we not only enjoyed but that helped to define us. That we aimed so high and dreamed so creatively spoke well of the spirit our parents had cultivated in us. They fought the "clouds of inferiority" that the Rev. Martin Luther King said formed in the minds of black children. We could do whatever we wanted and go wherever we wanted just as long as we made the right choices. My parents, my neighborhood, and the great history and traditions of Wichita helped me make these choices.

A person could backstroke in all of the Barry Sanders lore floating out there in the pop culture sea. Can you separate the fact from the fiction in the following tales?

◆ He once swallowed a straight pin he used as a toothpick and had to sit out a game his sophomore year in high school
◆ During two-a-day practices in high school, he attended the first practice, spent the day roofing with his father in hundred-degree heat, and then returned for the evening practice
◆ For a brief period, he averaged 30 yards per carry in high school
◆ He can throw a football with either hand
◆ When he was younger, he could dunk a basketball from a flat-footed stance under the basket
◆ He could eat a loaf of bread in one sitting
◆ He had a dog that ran the length of the football field during a halftime show at a Wichita State University home game
◆ He once played electric football for sixteen straight hours
◆ He frequently found himself standing in the corner of Ms. Boyd's third-grade classroom, holding a stack of dictionaries, and standing on one leg
◆ He'd obnoxiously honk like a goose in class behind the teacher's back

It can be difficult to separate the real from the surreal with Barry, but I know the man. The Barry I know stayed up late into the night to help me piece together the bicycle I needed to get to and from summer football workouts in high school. He knew how much I wanted to play. He's the person who, before sports fans swooned at the mention of his name, offered to split his grant money with me when he learned that I was struggling to stay in college.

He's the intellectually curious man who, as he's reading a book, copies definitions of words he doesn't know in an accompanying notebook for future reference. He's the generous friend who has exposed me to so much (from the Cannes Film Festival to Copacabana Beach in Rio de Janeiro) and opened so many opportunities (such as helping him write this book) that I couldn't begin to repay him.

He's the philanthropist who cares about people's struggles and relishes the prospect of helping people and then retreating so as not to draw attention to himself. He's the friend who'd rather march in your parade than lead his own. The Barry I know loves to laugh.

The truth is—all of these stories are true. It has been amazing to see him move from the roughhousing boy I knew back on Volutsia Avenue to the savvy businessman and doting father he is today. In Barry's case at least, all the lore and urban myth in the world can't hold a candle to the truth about him as a person.

Mark E. McCormick, Life-Long Friend

2

MOTHER

I would not have been as successful in football without the help of my mother, Shirley Sanders. I don't think she knows much about how to break down defenses, and she never once instructed me on the mechanics of taking a hand-off or making defenders miss, but she may have been my finest coach.

I've never seen her emotionally shaken. I have never seen her lose it. I have never seen her discouraged to the point where she wanted to give up. She was a strong and resilient person with great emotional balance. As a player, I could sense her composure in my approach to the game. Through her I learned to develop the resilience and balance I used on the field. A friend of mine told me that Tiger Woods' mother—and her Buddhist influence—might hold the key to Tiger's success. Tiger's ability to summon a deep calm under pressure separates him from his peers. The same

is true for my mother. She gave me the ability to stay calm under pressure.

Many times in my playing career, if not most of the time, I faced defenses designed to stop my team's running game. The other team had eleven players on the field focused mostly on playing the run and targeting on me. On a lot of plays, they had some success shutting me down. They'd manage to wall me in, swarm me, hold me to a yard or two, or even stop me behind the line of scrimmage. And they wouldn't simply try to stop me; they'd try to demoralize me. Discourage me.

Late in the game, my stat sheet would read something like: 1 yard, 1 yard, 2 yards, 0 yards. But I'd keep coming, play after play, quarter after quarter. Then, somehow, I'd find a way to exploit some small error—a missed tackle, a poor pursuit angle— and sixty yards later, I was handing the ball to the ref. Mother raised us that way: to be faithful; to keep pushing; to not give up; and to smile along the way. Those qualities served me well on the field and in life.

Her tenacity was just one of the gifts she gave to me. She is also the genealogical benefactor I should thank for my heavily muscled legs, my most valued asset as a player. I got my build from her side of the family, the Fishers. I've always been told, especially by my sister Nancy, that I have "Fisher legs," meaning muscled quads and calves.

My maternal grandfather, Johnny Fisher, also had big calves. Grandpa Fisher was a brick mason who inspired awe and respect in my father by once going to work on a broken leg. He just propped up his leg and continued laying bricks. I can see him in my mother. She has an incredible gift for

tenderness, but she also has toughness. She ran our home that way.

Throughout my childhood, we had a decent meal everyday, but I never remember her sitting down to eat. She was always taking care of us. In fact, she rarely got to have anything for herself. She used to like to drink Dr Pepper, and sometimes she'd go off somewhere in the house to try to enjoy one. All of us kids would be in the den, but when we heard that top pop, we'd all converge on her for a sip. It never seemed to bother her. She had a way of endlessly giving without appearing as if we were taking from her or that our requests taxed her at all. Mother cares about everyone who comes in contact with her. She cares about what they're going through and what they're facing on any given day. A lot of people can act like they care about the concerns of other people, but she really does care.

All of her strength comes from her faith in God. When I was young, she'd get up every morning and pray, and on many nights, we'd have a big family prayer. We all would sit in a circle and each of us in turn would say a brief prayer, and then we'd finish with "The Lord's Prayer." Her faith was the source of what we saw as an endless supply of patience and kindness.

But she was no pushover.

As is the case with most teenagers, I often wanted to hang out with my friends on Friday night. One time I asked her if I could go out with them, having done it the previous week.

She said, "No, you're not going to do that."

The same thing happened when I

I always feel good when I'm with my mom. Here we are on the bench at the Pro Bowl.
Page 17: **We're posing for the camera at home in Wichita.**

asked her if I could get a BB gun. Everyone had one, and I wanted one, too.

"No," she said. "We're not having any guns in this house."

After she said "no" in a certain way, I knew there was no more negotiating about it. She said it the way it needed to be said. Sometimes you knew you could explore why she felt that way, and sometimes you knew not to say anything more. When it came to things like sleepovers at a friend's house, she was actually quicker to say "no" than my father. She wanted to know where we were and who we were with so that she wouldn't

have to worry about us.

And if there was any worrying to do, she wanted to do it. She still makes us feel safer when we're with her, but that feeling was especially strong when we were kids. She was the shelter. I'm sure it was difficult running that household and taking care of all of us, but she wanted that burden on her own shoulders. She wanted to make sure that whatever was happening became her struggle, not our struggle.

I remember picking up the phone once when I was a child and the guy on the other end said that if he didn't receive the

BARRY SANDERS

overdue house payment something bad was going to happen. But I don't recall ever feeling we were in danger of being kicked out. My mother wanted to protect us from such things, and she didn't let us know when she was worried about those things. I think she loved her role as mother and protector.

She grew up in a similar family. She was raised in Wagoner, Oklahoma, which is little more than a cluster of tiny homes clinging to the rolling prairie near Tulsa. She was the oldest of eleven children, and so she was almost a second mother in that home, inheriting a number of maternal duties in addition to her own set of chores. Winter on the plains can be particularly harsh. Lashing winds slice their way over the flat landscape, and Mother spent many such days having to leave school in those winds to feed the family's hogs.

She met Daddy when they were both students at Horace Mann Junior High School, after her family moved to Wichita. At nineteen, she married the sweet, industrious little boy who always had a job and who always had money enough to offer her candy. She eventually had eleven children of her own. I was the seventh. She raised us, took us to church, cooked, cleaned, and somehow had the focus and the drive to return to school and earn a nursing certificate from Wichita State University.

Through the years, our relationship has matured seamlessly. There was never a time when we suffered an abrupt change between us. Only now, as I look back from the perspective of being an adult and a parent,

can I see the subtle changes that did take place. As I grew up, she saw that I was changing from a boy into a man, and she treated me accordingly.

When I was at Oklahoma State trying to decide if I should enter the NFL draft, she advised me, giving me her opinion on what I should do, but she let me make the final decision on my own. Some parents are always going to see you as their child and feel that they have a right to tell you what to do. They have a hard time living with the fact that their kids are now grown.

But Mother is so insightful that she seemed to have been thinking about our relationship changing long before the changes occurred. There weren't any bumps. I always knew that I could tell her anything, and I knew that when I did tell her something the information was as safe as it could get. She wouldn't tell anyone.

I remember having to tell her that B.J., my first son, was on the way. I felt strange telling her the news, because I was not married to B.J.'s mother. I knew I had to tell her about B.J. as well as about the decision not to get married. She was surprised, and I'm sure she was a little hurt, though she didn't express those feelings. She took the news in her usual calm way.

I see her influence in my everyday life, and she has shaped the way I view the world: Try to be considerate of other people and put everything into your kids. It must work for her. I've rarely seen her discouraged or unhappy.

Daddy and Mother stand beside me with the Heisman Trophy.

NOW YOU SEE HIM

3

I'M NOT YOUR FRIEND,
I'M YOUR FATHER

My daddy sat in his easy chair, a University of Kansas basketball game flickering on the projection-screen television in front of him. My son Nigel, four months old at the time, sat in his lap, staring in the direction of the screen, as if he could follow the Xs and Os of the game. Daddy's calloused palms tenderly covered the baby's tummy and chest. Now and then, Nigel would squirm or squawk, and Daddy would offer a firm but gentle, "Hey, all right now."

As we chatted on that January evening about the Jayhawk chances for the season, it occurred to me that until the previous November, just two months before, we hadn't talked for an entire year. Until a confrontation occurred in the kitchen of the house, just a room away from where we were sitting, he'd been the nuts and bolts of every part of my life. But in that year, I'd settled into retirement, gotten

engaged, gotten married, started a new career in business, and brought home my second son without him.

Yet here we sat talking sports while he held my son. Who'd have thought that some-one only twenty-one inches long could bridge all the miles of misunderstanding between my father and me? We obviously love each other, but in the preceding years and months, we collided like rams.

I sometimes wondered if I was ever quite the son he thought I should be. His way of raising us never made sense to me until recently. Daddy once said that most little boys have no fear when with their father. "A father could jump in a gasoline ocean with a torch in his ass and most little boys would jump in after him," he said. "But not Barry. Barry was always different."

I've been close to my mother for as far back as I can remember. I can recall clinging to her apron in our kitchen, following her from the fridge to the sink to the stove. When Daddy saw this, he growled that a boy shouldn't follow his mother around like that. Pretty soon, he said, I was going to be out working with him, where I belonged.

He terrified me at times. I've always maintained a healthy fear of him, starting with the day one of the kids in the house stole some quarters he'd kept in a shoe in his closet. When no one confessed, he lined all of us up and whipped us. I was five. My emotions toward him baffled me. I feared him, and I loved him, all at the same time. Many nights at the dinner table, I'd fume. My mother and my brother and sisters and I would all be sitting around the table, knives and forks in hand, a dish of sweet,

steamy food placed in the middle of the table—waiting. No one could eat until Daddy (a name we pronounced "Deddy") came home and sat down. And when he did, no one could speak. I never understood that.

He never understood me either. Daddy, from time to time, slept outside because he loved the outdoors. He'd sleep in our screened-in porch or on one of the picnic tables he'd hammered together in the backyard or right on the lush green lawn he clipped and edged with mathematic precision. He once asked me to sleep out there with him and I said, "No." I must have been seven or eight then. He couldn't believe it. It hurt him. It was as if I didn't love him or trust him. But as much as that may have hurt him, it was a footrace that never happened that wounded him much more deeply.

Mother said that Daddy still talks about it all these years later. Daddy was a fantastic athlete in his own right. He once was offered a tryout with the Oakland Raiders, but his growing family—I think he had three children at the time—prevented him from following through. That's likely why he always was so harsh in his attitude toward girls and us having girlfriends, but that's another story. Daddy was a very fast runner. He could outrun us for short distances—him running backward and us running forward—until we got to high school. But a friend of mine, Derrick Parker, beat Daddy one day. And Derrick didn't just beat Daddy; he strutted around and teased him afterward.

Daddy was furious. It got so bad that Daddy made my brother Byron race Derrick, but Derrick beat Byron, too. I was a couple

Above: **Daddy leans on a counter at the Barry Sanders grocery in Wichita.** *Page 23:* **I watch my son Nigel, who was a surprising catalyst for a reconciliation with my father.**

of blocks away shooting baskets at an out-door court when one of my cousins ran up and told me that Daddy wanted me to come home and race Derrick. I said, "No."

I felt really uncomfortable. Daddy didn't wear embarrassment well. The whole incident hurt his pride. But I just couldn't see going back and racing Derrick for that. I have competitive fire, but this just seemed ridiculous. He later said that if anyone had beaten his father and then strutted around afterward, he'd make the guy race him until he'd saved face for his father. Or, he'd fight the guy. He said he loved his father that

much. I can only imagine what he must have thought of me when I decided not to race.

That was the first time I had refused a specific order from him. But over the next few years, the air between us would crackle from the tension. One of the worst moments came shortly before the NFL draft deadline when Daddy cornered me and cussed me out for even considering staying at Oklahoma State for my senior year. I'd never seen him that way, so emotional. He was right in my face, screaming. He was almost in tears. I relented, obviously, and entered the draft.

Daddy stretches his arms proudly around the Heisman Trophy. He put the trophy in his friend's restaurant, where it remained for a while.

Through the money I made in my career, I was able to do things for him that I'd always wanted to do. He'd spent years climbing up and down ladders carrying circular saws and enormous flaps of shingles on a back that forty pounds of pressure should have snapped. With the money I was able to give him, he didn't have to do anything. He had no bills, a sprawling home on a man-made pond, and several vehicles. He could travel when and where he liked. But whatever I gave him never seemed to be enough. When I decided to set a limit, he exploded.

In the kitchen, in the home I'd bought for him in Wichita, he was bitterly explaining to me what I should be doing

with my money. Much of that "advice" had to do with giving him more of it. Our relationship was at stake, he said, and before leaving the room, he approached me menacingly. That was the last time we would speak for a year.

Two weeks before my wedding, I invited him to Las Vegas for a fundraiser. I wanted to talk to him. I needed his advice. I needed him to be there with me. But he decided not to come and then conspicuously skipped my wedding. Looking back, I can see that the whole episode was a function of the changes within our relationship.

I remember one day, for example, when I was walking with him and a young man I'd hired to care for the lawn at his house. We were walking the property line, and Daddy was pointing here and there, explaining how he wanted things done. Before long, talking almost exclusively to the young man, he launched into a painful story about his past.

He said when he was young, he had dreamed of being a printer. He read books about it and prepared himself for a career by picking up odd jobs. He eventually landed a job as a printer, but being the industrious teenager he was, he also worked as a janitor at the Air Force base. When he arrived late to deliver plans for a printing job, he found a "closed" sign in the window, and went on to his next job. He found out later that despite the sign the customer had still been waiting for him inside. Daddy was fired the next day. He said he thanked God that every time he lost a job, he got a better one, but he told the story in a way that made it clear that he still felt cheated. I had never heard that story, and I wondered why he was willing to open himself so earnestly to a stranger, and yet he had never shared the story with a son who loved him. Then I thought of something he told Byron and me once: "I'm not your friend, I'm your father."

One of my father's faults was that he was unable to see our conflicts for what they were: healthy. As painful as it was, it was healthy. It was the way it should have been. Separation. That's the word. At some point a child must separate from the parent and begin to live his own life and make his own decisions. We don't always choose when that time comes. Sometimes it can be harder for the parent than for the child. I think I now can understand why it was so difficult for him.

His life was difficult. He was preparing his children for the 1937 world he was born into as a black man. It was a tough world. It was mean. It was unfair. And, at times, he was all of those things to us. But what I now understand is that he was making sure that we would face nothing out in the world that he hadn't prepared us for. People think they know him, but they don't. They have no idea how significant he is. They see the proud father grabbing the microphone, filling the reporter's notebooks, and soaking up the glow of his son's celebrity. But those sound bites lie about his significance.

Daddy makes the world work. He takes care of his family, worships God, and contributes to his community as a good neighbor. He loves people, he loves to laugh, and his friends say he's one heck of a friend. You can't know him unless you're around him. Unfortunately, people only get to know him in those lying sound bites. They don't know how significant he is, but I hope he knows how important he is to me and to the family. He laid the groundwork for who I am. He's been a part of every part of my life. He was the difference between me and the many talented athletes who had shimmering futures in the palms of their hands and squandered them in bottles of alcohol and snootfuls of white powder.

Coming to my Little League games, coming to school, taking me to work with him—those things will follow me from now on and will help shape the lives of my children. It is hard to express his significance to me, but I'm reminded of it now with the feeling I have when I'm able to watch him with Nigel.

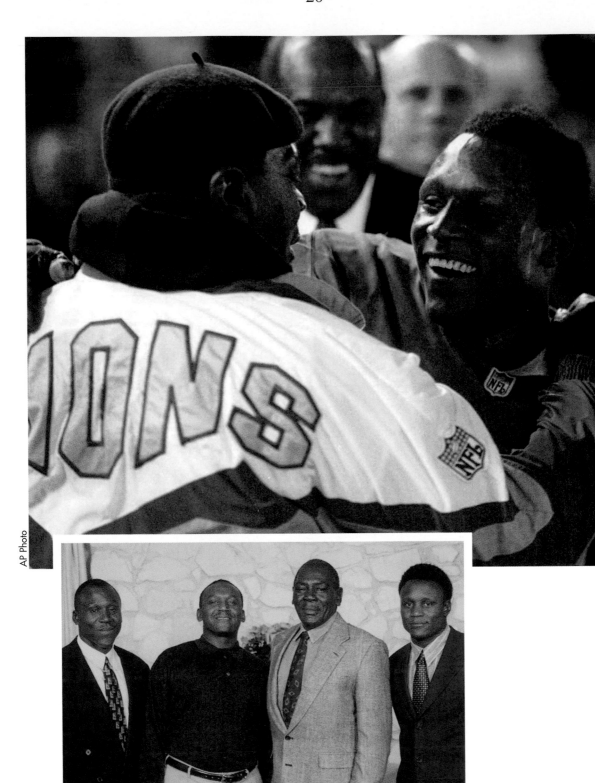

BARRY SANDERS

Clockwise from bottom left:
(l-r) **My brothers Boyd and Byron, Daddy, and me; Daddy hugs me on the sideline after I broke the 2,000-yard mark; Daddy sits among my sisters,** *(l-r)* **Krista, Elissa and Gina; Daddy with me on the sideline at a Pro Bowl game.**

4

YOUNG, ALIVE, AND
A REDSKIN

I guess that everyone hides a bit of insecurity. I'm not talking about the whiny, wimpy form of insecurity but a healthy concern about one's own limits, an awareness of the boundaries and the outermost confines of abilities. Without those concerns, without that focus and attention, how can you ever push beyond them? How do you keep from resting on what you've already accomplished?

My challenge always has been my stature. From the time I played Little League ball, coaches didn't think that I measured up. Some played me, others benched me, but virtually everyone doubted me. And that's saying something in Little League, where the players usually weigh only fifty or sixty pounds. But I was small even for my age. I often held the title of smallest on the team.

That's me in the front row, third from the right. My brother Byron is in the middle of the second row, number 44. That's me on the previous page, too, smiling and probably thinking about sports.

In early elementary school, when everyone was roughly the same size, I played quite a bit, and I played quite well. Though I was small, I also was faster than most everyone and showed it on the field in a number of long touchdown runs. But when everyone continued to grow except me, it got more and more difficult to get any playing time. One coach wouldn't play me because I had a heart murmur—a gurgling sound in my heart caused by irregularly closing heart valves. Most murmurs are not dangerous, but they can be caused by blood flowing through a damaged or overworked heart, and valve disease may result. When Daddy found out the reason I wasn't playing, he was angry. He pulled me out of school to go to the hospital for a battery of tests that turned up nothing. Doctors gave me the go-ahead. But the coach wouldn't budge. Despite the fact that I was good enough to play, I sat the bench a lot. He just thought I was too small and wanted to start someone else, a fantastic player in his own right—a guy named Kenneth "Dabby" Dawson, who went on to play at the University of Wyoming. I would play against him in the 1988 Holiday Bowl.

Don't get me wrong. There were good players on the team who deserved to start, but I deserved some playing time, too. Maybe it was my size or maybe it was the heart murmur. To this day, I don't know.

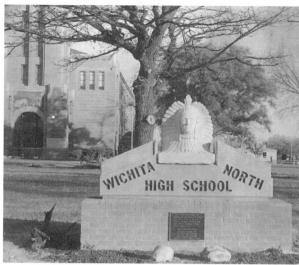

Clockwise from above: **A view of Wichita North High School; a shot of me in my Redskin football uniform; homecoming king; playing on the North basketball team.**

NOW YOU SEE HIM

BARRY SANDERS

WICHITA NORTH

High school wasn't a lot different. I attended Wichita North and was proud to be a Redskin. I started at tailback on the sophomore team, but in my junior year my brother Byron started at tailback and was outstanding. That year, the varsity coach, Bob Shepler, recognized my speed and started me at defensive back. I also returned punts and kickoffs. By returning punts, kicks, and interceptions to the end zone, I led the team in touchdowns that year.

Because of that success, in my senior year I expected to start at tailback. Byron had graduated, and I had proven I could run. Instead, I started as a wingback, basically a wide receiver, while a talented underclassman named Orlando Parker got the tailback position. Coach Shepler had moved on to become the athletic director, and we had a new coach, Dale Burkholder, but I found out later that Parker was Shepler's choice. Shepler thought I was too small for the position and told the new coach not to put me at tailback. He also had another complaint about me—he thought I lacked "contact courage," meaning I was afraid of being hit, afraid to run directly into the line or into a defender. Two other coaches on the staff said that Shepler mentioned to them that I had a yellow streak up my back.

He apparently came to that conclusion based on my spit-on-a-hot-skillet running style. Shepler wanted backs to run to an assigned spot whether a hole had opened there or not, but I'd get the ball and move like a tremor wherever I could find cracks in the defense. To be fair, the coaching staff probably hadn't seen anyone with my combination of physique and running style. There weren't a lot of role models.

However, Coach Burkholder, whom we called "Coach B," recognized my unique abilities and eventually would move me in as the starting tailback. Coach B was new-school and Shepler was old-school. Coach B cracked jokes and made his sometimes difficult practices fun. He was all enthusiasm. Before practice, and sometimes during drills, he would chant "It's great to be young, alive, and a Redskin."

Before the first game, Coach B closed us up in a gymnasium until it was time to board the team bus. He wanted us to meditate, concentrate, envision what we were about to do. We all spread out on the floor of the darkened gym. Some people relaxed quietly, others mumbled to themselves, some fell asleep.

Not me.

I couldn't sit still. The insecurity bug nibbled at me. My heart thumped under my pads. I got up. I sat down. I walked around. I looked out the door. I sat down again. I just wanted to get it over with—to get on the bus and get to the field and start the game. One of the reasons I stopped running track as a kid was that I hated those endless, tension-filled times before the race. The pressure was simply overwhelming.

But whatever doubts I felt that night were unfounded. I scored on four dramatic runs, racking up 157 yards off gadget plays from my wingback position. That's thirty yards per carry. After the game, I'm certain Coach B wanted to move me to tailback, but he was meeting resistance from Shepler. It was the size thing again, as well as his concerns about my "contact courage."

Above: **Game photos—running for the Redskins.**
Below: **Posing with Coach B in 1991.**

Coach B finally pulled the trigger going into our fourth game of the season, which was against South High. I think that game offered the first glimpse into the kind of running back I would become. I rang up 274 yards and four touchdowns, not including a fifty-yard reception called back because of a penalty. Coach B showed the team a tape of one of my scoring runs, and I could hardly believe it was me. I owe God a lot of thanks for blessing me with the gift to run that way.

The play started with a simple toss to the right, but that run had more stops and changes of direction than an airport flight line. I took the toss and drifted to the right, drawing in the defense, veering away from a lineman who had already crossed the line of scrimmage. When I reached the corner, the tight end was still on his man to my outside shoulder, but four other defenders closed from the left. Sensing they were approaching too quickly, I stopped abruptly, cut left, and watched them tumble into each other. I swiveled out of the cut and turned up field, but having come to a complete stop, I'd given a linebacker time to almost catch me. I stopped again and then jumped. His momentum carried him past me, his arm on my waist, his cleats airborne. Changing direction in the air, I darted forward.

The first set of defenders who had run past me now had recovered, and they were rushing toward me. I bolted up field with a fast defender out ahead of me and to my right, bearing down on the area between the hash marks and attempting to cut off my

NOW YOU SEE HIM

path to the end zone. I put on a burst and flashed past him before he could cut me off, and then flicked off the last defender with a stutter-step and trotted into the end zone. After the game, Coach B told reporters that the play showed my natural acumen for running the ball.

"It was one of the greatest runs I've ever seen by a high school running back," he said. "I said, 'My Lord.' Not many people

I'm standing with Coach B and his daughter Erin at the 1986 Kansas Shrine Bowl, an annual high school all-star game.

It was the last game of our senior season, and we were winning the ball game. I pulled a lot of the starters, but Barry was in a battle for the city rushing title. In the fourth quarter, we were on the sidelines, and I called him over to ask if he wanted me to put him back in the game so he could get enough yards to win the title. I said, "I can either put you back in or let the young kids play." In the blink of an eye he said, "Let the young kids play, coach." That's Barry.

I wish every coach had the experience of working with a talent and with a kid like Barry Sanders. He was special, a person with a lot of character. He was a quiet kid, never said much, and never gave an excuse. I remember he missed the first practice, and I had to discipline him. He told me he had to finish a construction job with his dad and that he was sorry and wouldn't miss again. One thing about Barry Sanders— you can believe him. He's very true to his word. And he was always willing to play hurt. It bothered me when I would hear, after he made it to the pros, that he wouldn't play hurt. I know different. He would play hurt all the time. He'd lay out for passes that other players would just let go.

He was a team kind of guy. He liked being on a mission with a group of guys. When the team ran out onto the field, you were going to see Barry in the middle of a big group. He wasn't going to be the first guy through the bust-away.

He was a very easy player to coach. He was a stickler for the fine points, and he loved being shown. He loved being coached. He was always eager to improve his game. I remember watching him as a pro and saw he was still working to improve even in his final year. When he was in high school and college, he wasn't a blocker, not that you want a runner like that to do a lot of blocking. But as a pro he steadily improved that part of his game. He'd put his head right into a rushing linebacker.

In fact, because he was such a stickler, I could tell in his last year or so that he was losing enthusiasm for the game. When he took a handoff, he was just reaching for the ball with both his hands down. He wasn't keeping his elbows high. That showed me that he'd lost some of his focus.

At North, I imitated the University of Nebraska offense—a Nebraska slot I. We started the season with Barry at the wingback, but in the first game he scored three times on the wingback reverse. I already had a good player at the I, but Barry was just too good not to put there. No one could tackle him. He wasn't a traditional runner. He ran scared, but that's a pretty damn good way to run. When Barry got the ball, he made things happen.

Dale Burkholder, Head Coach, Wichita North

BUT I WAS SMALL EVEN FOR MY AGE. I OFTEN HELD THE TITLE OF SMALLEST ON THE TEAM.

could ever do this. If they just went out in their front lawn and tried to do these moves, they'd probably hurt themselves." As he watched the videotape of the run, he said to a reporter, "Look at him reading his blocks, changing his speed. That's natural, God-given talent." His praise meant a lot to me, partly because he had coached Mike Rozier at a Kansas junior college. And he was right about owing my talent to God.

On the strength of such performances, I suddenly found myself in the thick of the race for the City League rushing title. You might think that I won that race, but I didn't. During our last regular-season game, Coach B told me I was close to the title. The leader in the rushing race was a blue-collar back named Brad Wiesen, who played for one of the two powerhouse Catholic schools in town. He had carried the ball thirty-nine times that night in his bid for the title. Nevertheless, the title fluttered within reach.

I asked Coach B if he thought that we'd put away East High, the team we were playing, and he said, "Yeah." In that game I already had gained 262 yards, including a 92-yard touchdown, so I told him to leave me on the bench and let some of the other guys

play. I cheered them on from the sidelines. Wiesen finished with 1,450 yards on 226 carries for a 6.4 yards-per-carry average. Despite not starting at tailback until the fourth game of the year, I finished with 1,417 yards on 139 carries, a 10.2 yards-per-carry average.

Had I won the rushing title before that point in the game, I would have been fine. I would have liked to win it. But to try to get it after the game was in hand seemed to me to lack dignity. I would do the same thing again as a rookie with the Lions. I was about eleven yards from the rushing title when I told the coach, Wayne Fontes, who wanted to put me back in so I could win the title, that I was fine on the bench. It wasn't that I was trying to be modest. It just didn't feel right to focus on an individual award rather than on what the team needed.

I finished the season with All-City and All-State honors, and even made Honorable Mention All-American. I was named the Most Valuable Player of the annual Shrine Bowl, a charity game showcasing the state's best prep players. You would think with a season like that, the questions and the doubts about me would ease.

Instead, they only grew.

5

COWBOY

Despite a great senior season in 1985 at Wichita North, almost no one recruited me and certainly not my beloved University of Oklahoma Sooners. Emporia State, Iowa State, Tulsa, and eventually Oklahoma State came calling, but I heard nothing from either of the big schools in the state—the University of Kansas and Kansas State University, both of which had programs so bad that they couldn't even beat each other. During one of their games in the late 1980s, they played to a tie, sending the home-field Jayhawk fans into a frenzy.

Ron Chismar, the coach at Wichita State University (which killed its program around the same time), had a year or two before recruited a friend of mine named Wes Anderson. He was compact and quick like me, but he had battled a string of injuries and wasn't producing enough for

Chismar. When asked why he didn't recruit me, Chismar reportedly said, "We don't need another midget."

That size thing again.

I finally decided on Oklahoma State, which had entered the recruiting race late. They were recruiting one of my high school teammates, Joel Fry, who was also quite a wrestler. While watching Joel's highlight reel, the Oklahoma State recruiter wondered who was zipping all over the field behind the blocks. The team figured I'd at least be a good kick returner.

At Oklahoma State, I quickly became my own man. Growing up in a family of eleven kids can make it difficult to find an identity, but now I had an apartment, a summer job bagging groceries, and a new and delicious sense of independence. But being your own man, finding yourself, and ascending to the next level of maturity can cost a great deal.

In my case, it put me on a collision course with my father. A huge conflict brewed. It began when the OSU recruiting coach came to the house on the day I signed the letter of intent. Daddy wouldn't speak to the coach, refusing to shake his hand, and left in anger, saying as he walked out the door, "I think he's making a big mistake." I was hurt

by that statement and confused. I didn't know what he meant.

Later, my friend Mark said Daddy told him I chose Oklahoma State in order to hide. At OSU I was playing behind Heisman candidate Thurman Thomas, and I had declined offers from Iowa State and Tulsa, where I would have been the featured back. The conflicts continued after I moved to Stillwater to play for the Cowboys. I was a good and obedient son, but I also was trying to become my own man. I found myself being forced to choose between my father's wishes, or rather, his commands, and my own sense of what was right and what was reasonable. Fortunately, Daddy changed his mind. By the time he dropped me off in Stillwater, he supported my decision. He attended all my games, just as he had attended my every sporting event since Little League. He was a strong supporter of the program and of me.

In many ways, it was the happiest time of my life. I was on my own for the first time. I loved the camaraderie and the locker-room atmosphere. I was comfortable in Thurman's shadow, even though he may not have wanted me there. I had heard that there were scouting reports warning defensive players against injuring Thurman for fear

Career Rushing Totals at Oklahoma State University

YEAR	ATTEMPTS	YARDS	AVERAGE	TOUCHDOWNS	LONG RUN
1986	74	325	4.4	2	28
1987	105	603	5.7	8	50
1988	344	2,628	7.6	37	89
Total	523	3,556	6.8	47	89

Above: **Waiting for the handoff.** *Left:* **A special OSU game program featuring me on the cover.** *Page 39:* **Running against the Nebraska Cornhuskers.** *Next page:* **Heading for the goal line against the Oklahoma Sooners.**

of having to face me. If I heard those rumors, I'm sure that he did, too. Those rumors, and his having heard them, actually bothered me, because Thurman was a great back and my teammate.

Soon enough, however, my comfort zone began to collapse. I rushed for 654 yards in 1987, my sophomore season, as Thurman's backup, and I was voted second-team All-American as a kick returner. Thurman earned All-American honors and headed for the NFL, leaving me as the team's featured back. I was moving from the shadows to the spotlight. Toward the Heisman.

THE HEISMAN

The Heisman Trophy was something that I had difficulty understanding. How can you pick one guy and say he's the best? In a team sport, how can one person be the best? The candidates usually are running backs and quarterbacks, but what about all the down linemen? Those feelings aside, I really did want to win the award. I just didn't want all of the attention that came with it. I love a challenge. I love proving myself.

In 1988, I put together a pretty good season. I broke at least twenty-six NCAA yardage and scoring records, and I set (and still hold) the season-average records for most rushing yards per game (232), most points per game (21), and most all-purpose yards per game (295). I had two 300-yard games, 39 touchdowns, and 2,600 yards. No other player in collegiate history at that time had more than one 300-yard game in his career. In that last 300-yard game, I pulled myself out with the single-game collegiate record within reach. For the season records, I

had 600 more yards and 19 more touchdowns than the next person in the record book. I opened two consecutive seasons with a 100-yard kick-off return. I also hold the record for multi-purpose yards in a season. Of course, none of these records would be possible without my teammates. I share any accolades with them.

Despite all of these statistics and records, there were doubters. Michael Wilbon, a sportswriter for the *Washington Post*, for example, told the Associated Press that he was voting for Rodney Peete of the University of Southern California or for Steve Walsh of the University of Miami for the Heisman. He said that I wasn't one of his top choices because I hadn't played at the same level of competition. He said my brother Byron, a 1,000-yard rusher at Northwestern, could do what I did had Byron played in the Big 8. "To gain 1,000 yards for Northwestern, you have to be Jim Brown to do that," he said. "I think Byron Sanders, if you switched them, would be identical to Barry."

Comments like that don't bother me. All I care about is my own assessment of my performance.

The announcement of the winner was scheduled for December 4, with the ceremony to be held in New York. I had a choice to make: attend the ceremony or stay with my teammates in Tokyo, where we were playing a game against Texas Tech. I chose to stay with the team, and ESPN beamed me into the Downtown Athletic Club for the announcement.

When I heard, "Barry Sanders, of Oklahoma State University," a smile curled

My sisters gather around me to pose with the Heisman Trophy. From left to right: there's Donna, Elissa, Krista, and Gina.

NOW YOU SEE HIM

I REALLY DID WANT TO WIN THE AWARD. I JUST DIDN'T WANT ALL OF THE ATTENTION THAT CAME WITH IT. I LOVE A CHALLENGE. I LOVE PROVING MYSELF.

The Heisman ceremony was an amazing collection of great players. *Above:* **I'm surrounded by Heisman winners from the past.** *On the left:* **With running great Earl Campbell.**

on my lips. Though it wasn't in my every waking thought, I really did want the award. After telling the national media that I'd prefer Rodney Peete, my eventual teammate in Detroit, win the award, I reversed field.

In the game against Texas Tech, I broke the single-season rushing record held by Marcus Allen, who I used to watch on television in awe of his running style. It was a great way to end the regular season. A few weeks later we met Wyoming at the Holiday Bowl.

At a $175-a-ticket dinner to receive the award, I told a reporter, "I had no idea the things that would follow winning the trophy. I'm happy I did win the award. And if I knew all these things [such as meeting Earl Campbell, Jim Plunkett, and Steve Owens] would follow, I might fight Rodney Peete for it."

I was surprised and grateful when I learned of the voting tally. I received 559 of the 721 first-place votes that were cast in the national balloting, eight times as many as Rodney. I finished with 1,878 total points, while Rodney ended up with 912 and Troy Aikman wound up third with 582. And I did it with no marketing campaign and little national television exposure. In a race dominated by big-school, big-market quarterbacks, I was playing in "an obscure corner of the prairie," in the words of the *Washington Post*. (I wasn't even on the cover of the Oklahoma State football program. I didn't appear in the book until page twenty-two.) Still, I didn't put myself in the same category as past winners, such as Billy Sims, Tony Dorsett, Marcus Allen, and Charles White. But everyone else did, and my stock was suddenly soaring.

ON TO THE NFL

I really wanted to return to Oklahoma State for my senior year. As I said earlier, I was very happy there. It was fun being in college, and I wasn't ready to leave it behind yet. I had been the featured back for only one year. I wanted to stay. That's what Mother wanted, too.

But the NCAA hammer was dropping on Oklahoma State for a variety of violations, which allowed me to leave early, and others were telling me that I needed to enter the draft in order to maximize my earning potential. It was a tough decision to make.

Perhaps worst of all, I got my first taste of what was to come in my relationship with my father. During the press conference at which I announced that I'd be staying in school, despite the NCAA sanctions, Mother told a reporter, "It would be his money anyway, as far as I'm concerned. I feel it is necessary to finish one thing before you go on to something else. That's important to me. And I think if there is money this year, surely there will be some next year also."

To which Daddy responded: "I'm not as broad-minded as Shirley. She's talking about his money. I say our money because I'm going to be one of his principal agents."

As my deadline for declaring for the draft approached, I got another dose of what was to come in my relationship with my father. I listened to Daddy for hours, literally hours, scream and curse at me for even considering a return for my senior year in Stillwater. I'd never seen him so emotional.

I folded.

Before I knew it, I was making that long drive to Denver for another press conference, this time to announce my plan to enter the NFL draft and to preside over the official end of my childhood.

6

THE ROOKIE

Entering the NFL was like entering a small room full of gunfire or like being trapped on the median of a busy stretch of seventy-five-mile-per-hour highway.

On April 24, 1989, the Detroit Lions chose me in the first round with the third pick in the draft, and I officially became a pro football player. But I didn't sign a contract until September 8th. The season opened a few days later, and since I'd sat out all of training camp, I wasn't prepared. I got my first whiff of what I'd face in the next ten years in the first game against the Phoenix Cardinals. We were trailing late in the third quarter when Coach Wayne Fontes sent me into the game. My first run as a professional went for eighteen yards.

Running a variation of only one play, I finished the day with seventy-one rushing yards and a touchdown on nine carries. It was a good start, but while out on the field, the differences between the college and the pro game shocked

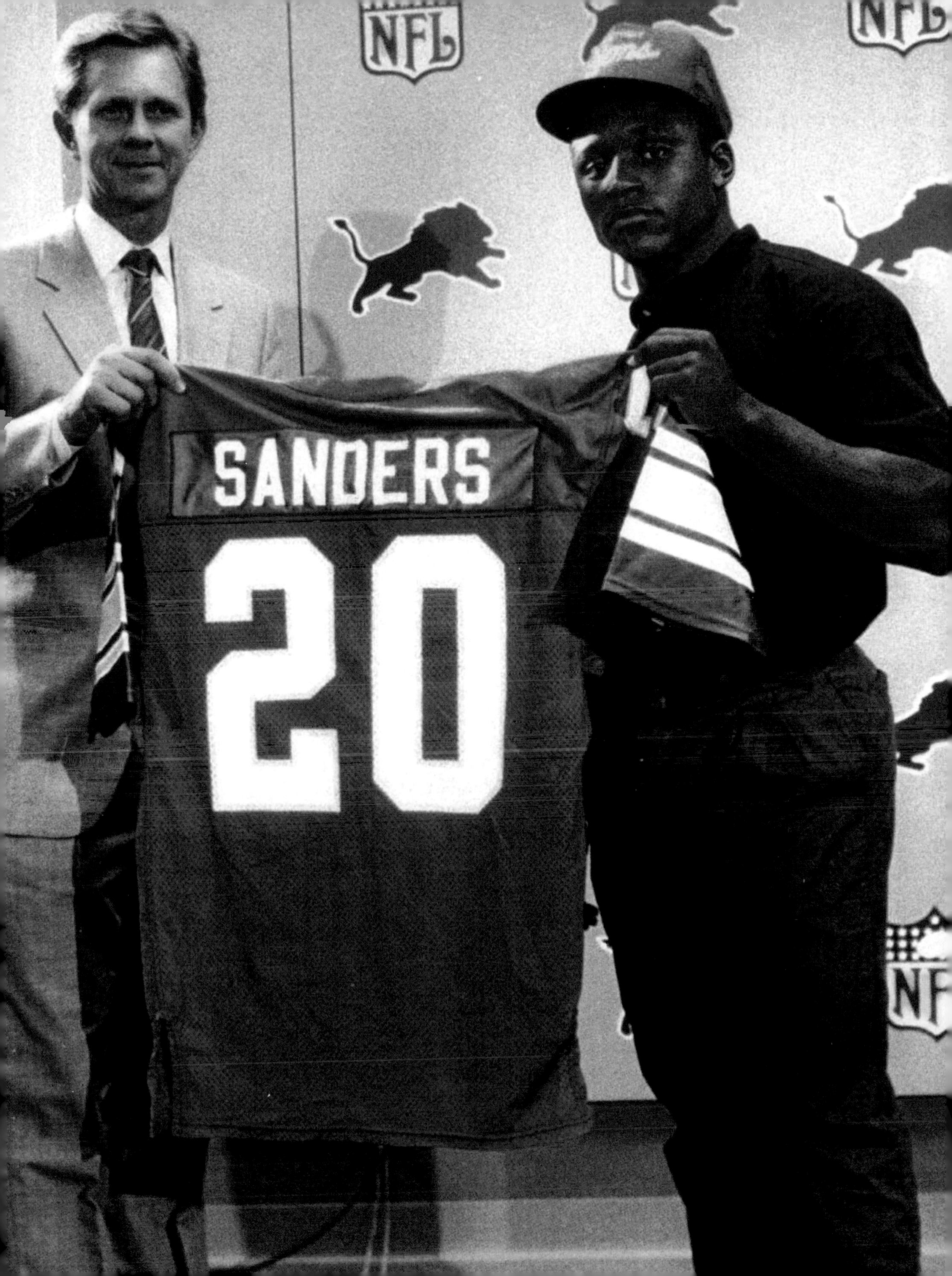
NFL
SANDERS
20
NFL
NFL

me. In college, you might face a defense with a couple of players with pro-grade speed, but in the NFL everyone is world class. Everyone, from the strong safety to the 300-pound lineman, moves quickly. In that first game it seemed like bodies were whizzing by me like bullets and colliding like cymbals. No one in their right mind would throw themselves off a roof over and over and over again, and yet that's what we did to our bodies once a week, nine months a year, until we left the game or until the game left us.

In what was then the NFC Central Division, I spent a lot of time on artificial turf. The pounding my knees took on that turf frequently caused them to swell, and the surface—basically pavement covered by a thin, green rug—just potato-peeled my forearms. My running style saved me from a lot of the calamitous shots that some backs and receivers took, but I did take a shot against the Bears in the third game of my rookie season that sidelined me with bruised ribs.

It felt great to be a professional player, a member of the NFL, but that was never my dream—not even close. When I was young I wondered if I was good enough to play college ball, and even then I just wanted to be competitive. I never thought I would stand out. Moving into pro ball, I felt the same way. I wanted to know if I could compete—not necessarily excel—on that level. Being there fed my natural curiosity as much as anything. I had always loved football, and now I was a screaming groupie suddenly allowed backstage.

I do think, though, that making it to pro ball was one of my brother's dreams.

CRUELLY CLOSE

One day Byron is in the spotlight as the star running back of Northwestern University, only the third player at the school to run for 1,000 yards in a season in the rugged Big 10 Conference. His name and face are all over the pages of the *Tribune* and the *Sun-Times* sports sections. He's drafted by the Chicago Bears and signs a two-year contract. He's so close to his dream.

But then the Bears cut him.

Only a few months removed from the wide streets of Chicago and all of that attention, he was back home in Wichita in his old room, grieving for the apparent end of his dream. I'm convinced that his collision with that fate was more violent than any he would have had to absorb in the league. It was a disappointment far deeper than most of us will ever experience.

I say that because so few of us get as cruelly and tantalizingly close to our dreams as Byron got to his, only to watch it dissolve. And he wasn't one of those empty dreamers, either. Too many people have dreams but place them on a shelf and stare at them longingly. Helplessly. They never put in the work that might bring the dream to life.

That's not true of my brother. He followed a muscle-bursting weight program. He jogged. He ran sprints. He studied nutrition and ate balanced meals. He ran stadium stairs. He maintained an impressive level of fitness year round and had done so for as long as I can remember. He wanted it so badly.

And it looked like he was going to get it. After graduating from North, Byron went to Hutchinson Community College for two

The Sanders brothers pose for a photo. Byron is on the left, Boyd in the middle, me on the right. *Page 49:* **I hold up my new Detroit Lions uniform for a photo with team general manager Chuck Schmidt.**

years, and then sat out a year because of a knee injury. He then transferred to Northwestern and gained 1,062 yards, tying Mike Adamle's school rushing record. Rather than return for his senior season, he wanted to turn pro, which he now feels may have been a mistake.

Despite his success at Northwestern, the Bears waited until the ninth round to take him with the 248th overall pick in the 1989 draft. A few weeks into training camp, they let him go. At the time he felt that he never really got a chance to prove himself. As time passed, he wondered if he wasn't ready, if he should have stayed for another season at Northwestern to prepare himself for pro ball. A few years after the Bears cut him, Byron got

a tryout with the Lions and with the World Football League, but he was cut again.

I could see the repercussions of that disappointment rippling through his life as the years past. First, he went back to college, where he earned a degree in human development and social policy from Northwestern in 1992. After graduation he searched for a career that would make him happy. But some college stars who don't make it in the pros take a few years to find their footing

He worked a two-year stint in Wichita as the head coach for a small Christian high school. He really seemed to grow within that role, but after that job, he still seemed lost. Even while he was at the

Wichita North retired Byron's and my jerseys—he was 48 and I was 3—in a ceremony that drew even the governor of the state.

high school, his teams played games at the Little League field named after me. But Byron always has been as compassionate as he is passionate. As a coach, he pushed the kids to push themselves, but he'd also drive to their homes to help them with their homework. In that way he was the helpful, gently guiding big brother Byron I'd always known.

You might think differently, but he never seemed bothered about the perception that he lived in my shadow. I think he has always been happy for me. I also think, however, that not casting a shadow of his own did hurt him. I have to say it was difficult for me, too, not simply because I care for him but because I've always been his biggest fan. I feel as if I share in his disappointments.

When we were children, I followed him from the basketball courts to the football fields and back. I wanted to do everything he did, and when my friends would invite me places I'd always ask if Byron could come along. It was a great moment when Wichita North retired my football jersey and retired Byron's, too.

I'm at the podium to say a few words about being drafted by the Lions. It was time to "Restore the Roar."

FIRST STUTTER-STEPS

If Byron's career was over, mine was just beginning. The on-field challenges intrigued and excited me, but the off-field challenges bored and frustrated me. Off the field, there were times when I felt that I didn't belong in the league. I signed autographs out of obligation, but I neither understood nor enjoyed it. I did like the handshakes and the photographs and the polite patter with the fans, especially children, but I was so green that I hadn't learned yet how to say, "Okay, I've signed enough of these. I need to get home or get to practice." I hated disappointing people, but I hated even more the sense that I could never get away.

Worse, I was learning lessons about the financial predators who target pro athletes. Try thinking of it this way: When you enter a crowded room, all you can see is the crowd. But you learn to consider the crowd as foliage or brush helping to conceal an attack in the form of a confidence scheme. Let's just say that many times when someone is patting you on the back, they aren't congratulating you, they're trying to get you to cough up something—like money.

On the field it was much different. I spent much of that first season dealing with a couple of nagging injuries, particularly a hip pointer that I suffered against the Bears. I had to play catch-up for most of the season when it came to learning the playbook—a phonebook-thick encyclopedia of our basic plays, sets, and philosophy. Having missed all of training camp, I was behind everyone else in learning the system.

At that time, the Lions used a complicated offensive attack called the Silver

Except for my parents and for my sister Nancy, Byron influenced me more than anyone else in my family. We were particularly close because of our ages. He's just a year older than me. We have an older brother, Boyd, but he had moved out of the house by the time that Byron and I were teenagers, and so we were the only boys in a house with eight sisters. During my early years in the NFL, Byron came to live with me. He seemed to be trying to find his way.

BARRY SANDERS

Stretch. The Silver Stretch was the pro version of an offense called the Run and Shoot, which was used by a couple of college teams. In that offense, the object was to spread out the defenders and attack them with quick passes to speedy receivers or with draw plays by the running back before the defense had a chance to react. All that space created by the spread-open defense gave me room to operate, to make people miss, and to rack up yardage.

The season took an interesting path. I didn't have a 100-yard game until the third game of the season, when we played the Bears. I had 126 yards on 18 carries in a little more than one half of the game. I had to leave the game with the hip pointer, which bothered me the rest of the year. Two games later, I gained 99 yards against the Vikings, making so many guys miss tackles that their coach, Jerry Burns, asked the officials to check my jersey. He thought I had sprayed it with silicon so no one could grab it.

I went off for 184 yards on 30 carries against Green Bay, and on Thanksgiving Day I

Left: **Trace Armstrong and Steve McMichael welcome me to the NFL.** *Inset:* **I'm kneeling on the sideline at my first Pro Bowl, talking to Randall Cunningham. That's Eric Allen next to him and Carl Lee on Allen's right.** *Above:* **It was a big thrill for me to have Billy Sims come onto the field to congratulate me for breaking his rookie rushing record.**

broke the 1,000-yard mark by gaining 145 yards against Cleveland. I think I earned a ceremonial turkey leg for that performance from TV analyst and former coach John Madden. Later in the year, I broke the rookie record for yards gained in a season, a record held by a former Lion who also had worn number 20: Billy Sims. Billy was at the game to congratulate me on the field, a great honor.

I received a number of honors for that first year: I was named first-team All Pro by the Associated Press, *The Sporting News*, the Pro Football Writers of America, *Football Digest*, and *College & Pro Football News Weekly*. A number of those publications and organizations, as well as a number of others, named me the NFL Rookie of the Year. I also made my first trip to the Pro Bowl.

I was fortunate to achieve so much success and must credit God and my teammates. I really wasn't aiming that high. I only wanted to be competitive.

NOW YOU SEE HIM

7

N A N C Y

The toughest person I've ever known wasn't Daddy, and it wasn't Lawrence Taylor, Howie Long, or John Lynch. The toughest person I've ever known was my sister Nancy, and the toughest thing I've ever had to endure was watching her fight a slow death. No one teaches you how to deal with something like that. You can't prepare for it. As we all do, I had to learn as I went, and even then I found myself wondering how there could be so much pain in the world.

The disease that killed Nancy is called scleroderma, a despicable condition that hardens and scars skin and connective tissues. It is one of a group of arthritic conditions with no known cause or cure. An estimated 300,000 people in the United States suffer from this condition, nearly four times more women than men. As it progressed in Nancy, we watched helplessly, as if watching a burning house collapse around her; only in her case, the house was her own body.

I watched this slow-motion implosion over the span of several years.

With Nancy, the disease began with what we thought were only patches of stubbornly dry skin. But soon, those patches began to get thicker and harder, and they started to spread to her hands, arms, face, and neck. Then, they started to scar and discolor.

Doctors say that there are two major forms of the disease: One form primarily affects the skin. The other, though, launches an all-out attack on not only the skin, but also on the lungs, the kidneys, and the gastrointestinal tract. Scleroderma leaves a person freezer-burned, inside and out.

My sister meant the world to me, and calling her "sister" doesn't capture her role in my life or her place in my heart. She was sister, mama, friend. Helplessly watching her suffer through the roller coaster of remission and collapse was perhaps the most agonizing episode of my life. The disease rotted her joints and inflamed them, making movement often blindingly painful.

It hardened her intestines to the point that she couldn't absorb nutrients, starving her. It hardened her lungs so that she couldn't breathe, strangling her. Most people fear drowning because of the suffocation. That's what this anaconda of a disease did to Nancy; little by little, it squeezed the life out of her.

But Nancy always seemed to have a quality that transcended life.

MEMORIES OF NANCY

I have a fond early memory of going with Mother to pick up Nancy from elementary school. She didn't go to the school we all attended or would attend when we were older. She'd been placed in a school for gifted and talented children. Most parents have to request that their child be tested as gifted and talented, but Nancy bloomed so brightly in the meadow of students that her teachers felt compelled to move her into a more challenging school.

Her accomplishments in school meant a great deal to me. It gave me an inner glow that she was such a good student, and made me feel special that she was so special. She always seemed to go out of her way to make me feel important. She'd decorate the house, for example, and throw birthday parties for me, and I don't remember her doing that for anyone else in the family. After my high school football games, she'd rally the family to paint banners and organize family parades for me.

Nancy always seemed to be there when I needed her. When I was about three years old, Mother took Nancy and me on a ride to where my daddy worked to bring him lunch. I was in Nancy's lap. Mother said when she turned a corner, the door of our old station wagon flew open, and Nancy and I were jolted out into the street. Either from fear or from pure instinct, Nancy wrapped me in a bear hug and made sure that when we hit the pavement, I landed on her. Mother says Nancy saved my life.

I always felt good being around Nancy, because she exuded a limitless capacity for giving. She was always working on some sketch or school project or church function. She was always trying to help people and to make herself a better person. She loved to sing, whether it was an aria from an

The entire Sanders family gathers for the photo above. *First row (l-r):* **Me, Krista, Donna, Gina;** *second row:* **Elaine, Mother, Gloria;** *third row:* **Diane, Nancy, Elissa, Byron;** *back row:* **Boyd and Daddy.** *Page 57:* **My sister Nancy.**

opera or a stirring gospel hymn. She loved to dance. She loved to sew her own clothes.

And she loved to laugh. She always seemed to be trying to make other people laugh, too. Her skits and imitations—inspired by Jerry Lewis and Gilda Radner—were rockets of creativity. We all laughed, especially when she imitated Daddy. But Radner was one of her particular favorites. I'd stay up with her to watch Radner on "Saturday Night Live." Nancy's favorite character on the show was Radner's Rosanne Rosannadanna. I really didn't understand the show or the comedy; I just enjoyed hanging with her.

One night a few years ago, I was flipping channels and caught a glimpse of a Gilda Radner biography—and burst into tears. When I saw Radner's image floating on the screen, I lost it. The image brought back many memories of Nancy, her creativity and her humor, her wonderful spirit. It also brought back the pain of watching one of the strongest people I've ever known being driven down, down, down by an incurable disease. She was trapped in a deteriorating body, and even with all of my muscles and money I could do nothing but watch. The fingers that filled our house with piano music were now stiff and

Nancy's funeral was held at the Paradise Baptist church on November 12, 1991.

wracked with arthritic pain. The arms that held me when we tumbled from the car were often folded uselessly in her lap. The person who'd boldly hung "No Smoking" signs in the house (a not-so-subtle suggestion to Daddy and his cigars) and taught me about the importance of standing up for myself found it physically painful to stand up. It was tough watching life so cruelly stolen from someone who not only wanted to give but who also had so much *to* give.

Despite what happened to her and the way she suffered, I can't feel sad without feeling as if I'm betraying her somehow. She would want me to be strong, to move for-

ward. Nancy spent much of the last year of her life with me in Detroit, moving in to my place in the summer of 1991. She'd already been ill for some time, but I didn't know much about the disease and asked her once, somewhat offhandedly, about the odds that she would overcome it.

"Fifty-fifty," she said. At that moment, I felt a creeping fear rise from my stomach to my throat.

Despite those odds, she handled herself with her usual courage. She enrolled at Langston (Oklahoma) University in a master's of music program. That took a lot of guts because little by little, I could see the disease chipping away at her. She could still drive, but walking became difficult. She tired easily. The pain was getting worse.

But she handled it so well. She didn't want anyone to feel sorry for her, and she wouldn't let anyone do anything for her that she could do herself. She knew she was going to die, but she said that if she died later rather than sooner, she'd have her master's degree in music. She was so strong. It was as if she were fighting off the deliberate march of the disease in order to give all of us time to come to terms with it, understand it, and say our good-byes.

She drove home to Wichita from Langston one weekend, not feeling well. When she arrived, she felt worse, and my sisters called for an ambulance.

She died at the hospital.

I was preparing for a game in Tampa Bay against the Buccaneers when my little sister Krista called to tell me that Nancy had died. I remember thinking to myself, in the midst of the pain of losing her: Could you have done more? Surely there was something else you could have done. But then I thought: She wouldn't have let me do more. It wasn't worth dwelling on anyway. It's better to remember her zest for life.

My appreciation for the arts comes from Nancy, too. Every time I've seen a play, I've thought of her. She always saw me as being someone better than I thought I could be. Had she been with me, I'd have laughed a lot more over these past ten years. I'd probably be a little wiser. I'm sure I'd be a better person.

But I can't be sad about the twenty-seven years of her life, much of which I got to experience. It was a gift, a blessing, a joy, and a privilege. I was fortunate to be her brother. A newspaper reporter wrote in Nancy's obituary that Williams Sanders says if you think his son is tough, you should have known his daughter Nancy.

How true.

NOW YOU SEE HIM

8

THE ROAR RESTORED

Success often seems to arrive in spite of something and often on the far end of probability. You win, sometimes, in spite of injuries. You win in spite of controversy that threatens team focus. You win in spite of general adversity.

In 1991, our team had all three, but we fell just one game short of the Super Bowl. We closed the season with a record of 12-4, nearly achieving what Coach Fontes imagined when he began his plan to "Restore the Roar" in Detroit. It was the most exciting year of my career. I never would have guessed that things would have turned out that way, given how badly things began.

I'll explain.

Shortly after the 1990 season ended, I'd asked the Lions to restructure and renegotiate my contract, and the situation began rotting from there. The Lions resisted, and I dug in, too. Month after month passed without a resolution. As the '91 season approached, it appeared that I'd be holding out of training camp.

In the meantime, I was being sued for a business investment involving a highway truck stop in Kansas. When the planned soured, everyone started looking for someone to sue, and before I knew anything, everyone was looking at me.

I sat out nearly the entire training camp before settling my contract dispute, and then I badly bruised my ribs in a preseason game with the Kansas City Chiefs. By the time our opener against the Washington Redskins rolled around, my ribs were so sore I could barely run. I couldn't twist my trunk at all without a belt of pain squeezing the breath out of me. I sat out the game, and it appeared that the rest of the team, did too. We lost 45-0, our worst defeat since Dallas pounded us 59-13 in 1968, the year I was born.

Coach Fontes shagged the questions reporters threw at him about my injury. "He told the coaches he was tightening up during the pregame meal, and I watched him work out prior to the game," Wayne told the press. "He was running gingerly, and he decided he couldn't go."

I guess the questions persisted, because he then added, "I think Barry is a tough back, but any player who tells me he can't play, then I won't play him. Barry is a unique talent, and the season isn't going to be won or lost in one game."

The timing, of course, could not have been worse. I was fresh off a hold-out and then I sat out a game in which we posted an historic loss to open the season. I also began to hear whispers about my toughness.

But winning is the antidote to just about any set of problems that might face a professional football team. We went out and won the next five games, going into the bye week at 5-1. After the week off, our fortunes went up and down. We lost, then won, then lost two more. Our problem mostly stemmed from injuries. As the season progressed, we lost starting quarterback Rodney Peete, linebacker Mike Cofer, nose guard Jerry Ball, and linemen Mike Utley and Eric Sanders.

THUMBS UP

Losing Mike Utley was the most frightening experience I'd ever had on a football field. It happened during our November 17 home game against the Los Angeles Rams. During a play, Mike fell forward, and the top of his helmet got caught on the turf, cracking his neck. His spinal cord was damaged beyond repair.

We didn't know the seriousness or the nature of his injury at the time. We all just stood there, eyes wide, breathing softly and waiting impatiently for him to get up. It seemed like we stood there for an hour. Before long, players from both teams had joined hands, knelt right there on the field, and prayed. A

Previous page: **I'm doing my best to avoid a tackle from Bears defender John Mangum.** *Opposite page:* **Mike Utley is wheeled away on a stretcher after his spinal cord injury. His courage in the face of tragedy united and inspired the team.**

Lomas Brown and I give the thumbs up on either side of Huddles, the mascot for Lions' charities.

nervous murmur vibrated through the crowd as emergency medical staff hovered over him. I'd always said, even in college, that all of my success could end in one play. Mike's injury was the first time I'd actually seen anything close to that happen.

As he was being wheeled away to applause, he raised his thumb, detonating a wild burst of cheers that literally turned the season around. We went on to beat the Rams that day, 21-10, and we won the next five games to finish the season at 12-4, the franchise's best record since a Lions team went 11-3 way back in 1962.

The team I played on in my first season was pretty good, and we won some games, ending up with a record of 7-9. Those numbers may not sound great, but we had finished well, winning six of our final seven games—the final five in a row—and so in my second season we were supposed to be pretty good. But we didn't play that well, ending up at 6-10.

Then, in that magical third season, we just got hot. We had a good combination of strengths. We had young guys who had a lot of fire. We had great special teams, and we had a good defense and an explosive offense. Seven players on that team were elected at the end of the season to play in the Pro Bowl: Jerry Ball, Bennie Blades, Lomas Brown, Mel Gray, Chris Spielman, and yours truly.

Until his injury, Rodney Peete was our quarterback. While he was hurt, Eric Kramer called the signals.

Otto Greule Jr/Getty Images

NOW YOU SEE HIM

Big Jerry Ball anchored our defensive line.

Jonathan Daniel/Getty Images

BARRY SANDERS

The year we had in 1991 was great, especially the way the team overcame the tragedy of Mike Utley's injury. That brought us together. In a way, the season just magically happened. We were young, and I guess we didn't know any better, and Wayne was the perfect coach.

But the key was Barry. Without the threat of a Barry Sanders, teams would have been bringing the house at us. But they couldn't come at us so hard with him in there, because they had to try to contain him. If I get into the Hall of Fame, it's because of him. He made it easier to keep my guy off the line.

At the same time, it was hard to block for Barry, because you didn't know where he was going to be. I might be assigned as the back-side tackle on a play, but then Barry would reverse field and go the other way, so I'd have to scramble and be the front-side guy. He wouldn't always go to the hole where you thought he was going. But when he had the ball in his hand, there was always a possibility he was going all the way, and we knew that when we were blocking for him.

That team was more like a family than any other one I was ever on. We opened our houses to each other, gave each other advice, really cared about each other. That chemistry was one of the reasons we were good. And everybody loved Barry. But when you invited him for dinner, look out. He could eat. One time he came over to my house with some Dove bars, and polished off three or four of them. Then my wife fixed him a full plate of food, and he ate that too. My daughters' mouths were hanging open watching him. He was a machine

He could sleep too. I used to tell him he had a sleeping disorder. He once fell asleep on the sideline during a game. He was sleeping with his helmet on. I told him that's why he started wearing that visor, so he could sleep on the bench and no one would know. He'd do that in meetings, too. As soon as the lights went off, Barry's head would start to nod. But he was able to get away with it.

Of course, he could have gotten away with a lot more. He was a superstar, but he didn't ever use that to get his way. He was a good person, a Christian, a lot like his mother. Jerry Ball and I used to say, "God blessed the right man. He knew who to give it to." If we'd had as much power as B (which is what we called him) we wouldn't have handled it as well as he did. Sometimes I wished he would have been more outspoken. We could have gotten a lot more things done there with management.

Chuck Schmidt, the general manager, didn't like when players tried to use their power. He felt threatened. That's why management ended up getting rid of so many guys on the team—Mel Gray, Bennie Blades, Jerry Ball, Chris Spielman, Brett Perriman, Willie Green, some others. Chuck was like that. But management knew Barry wasn't going to make any waves. He was so quiet and didn't seem threatening to anybody.

It's a shame they started tearing down that team. That playoff game in '91 shows you what we could have done. We beat Dallas, dismantled them, and they were similar to us. We were both young and building something. They went up from there, and where did we go? We could have won a Super Bowl. We could have won a couple of times. When I won the Super Bowl last year with Tampa Bay, I thought about all of those guys: Barry, Bennie, Kevin Glover, and the rest of them. I thought about what we could have done.

Lomas Brown, Teammate, Detroit Lions

I think we had been waiting on that team to show up for the first couple of years, and '91 it finally came together. We dedicated our season to Mike. We used his thumbs-up signal as our rallying point and went on to win the NFC Central Division title. We hosted and won our first playoff game in years by blasting the talented but rebuilding Dallas Cowboys 38-6. I don't think we realized that we were capable of such a game. If we did realize it, we certainly had never witnessed it. We ran the ball, we passed the ball, and the defense dominated.

We were a hair's breadth from the Super Bowl. We needed to win only one more game. Unfortunately, we needed to win it against the Washington Redskins. The Redskins were awesome that year. They finished at 14-2, the best record in the league. They led the league in points scored, and only the Saints had given up fewer points. The Redskins had annihilated us in the season opener. In the NFC Championship, it was just about as ugly as the first game.

I had 46 yards on six carries in the first quarter of that game and was forced to stay in the backfield and block Washington's blitzing linebackers. In the remaining three quarters, things got even worse. We fell behind 10-0 in the first four minutes of the game and trailed 17-10 at halftime.

In the third quarter, the dam burst, it seemed, literally and figuratively. We played in a cold, heavy rain, and our offense couldn't get untracked in the sucking mud, while the Redskins ran wind sprints through our defense. I finished the day with 44 yards on 11 carries. And it wasn't as if I wasn't trying. On one run I ran close to 80 yards for a simple 6-yard gain, running sideline to sideline.

"We had to work for everything we got," I told reporters after the game. And we didn't get much. The 41-10 loss disappointed us, but we lost to a great team. The Redskins went on to whip the Buffalo Bills in the Super Bowl, a game that my teammates and I had to watch on television like everybody else.

In later years, we'd show flashes of that team's talent and chemistry, but it would never quite come together the way it did in 1991. We'd have an explosive offense and a marginal defense, or a stingy defense and a plodding offense. Never both.

We also had more than our share of tragedies. Mike Utley would never play again. In June of 1992, a talented young lineman named Eric Andolsek was killed in a freak accident when a sleeping truck driver ran off the road and into Eric's front yard, running him down. Five years later, linebacker Reggie Brown would suffer a paralyzing spinal injury.

That NFL championship game was as close as I ever got to a Super Bowl in my ten years in the league.

NOW YOU SEE HIM

The 1991 Season Week by Week

Week	Opponent	Result	Score
1	at Washington Redskins	L	0-45
2	Green Bay Packers	W	23-14
3	Miami Dolphins	W	17-13
4	at Indianapolis Colts	W	33-24
5	Tampa Bay Buccaneers	W	31-3
6	Minnesota Vikings	W	24-20
7	BYE WEEK		
8	at San Francisco 49ers	L	3-35
9	Dallas Cowboys	W	34-10
10	at Chicago Bears	L	10-20
11	at Tampa Bay Buccaneers	L	21-30
12	Los Angeles Rams	W	21-10
13	at Minnesota Vikings	W	34-14
14	Chicago Bears	W	16-6
15	New York Jets	W	34-20
16	at Green Bay Packers	W	21-17
17	at Buffalo Bills	W	17-14

Postseason
NFC Divisional Playoff

	Opponent	Result	Score
	Dallas Cowboys	W	38-6

NFC Championship Game

	Opponent	Result	Score
	at Washington Redskins	L	10-41

9

AN UNEASY CROWN

It was as if the wide-eyed boy had driven his little toes through the tile floor of the grocery store. His mother tugged and pulled at him, but she might as well have been pulling on a fire hydrant.

The boy had spotted me.

I had just received a hero's welcome in Wichita that day as the city's first and only Heisman Trophy winner. There was a parade, rallies, and gifts from the mayor, including a key to the city. And when it finally was over, all I wanted to do was stop by a store and buy some Suzy Q's.

But as I was walking into the store, I noticed the little boy, who seemed to know who I was. He also seemed nervous, so I walked over and grabbed his hand and pumped it as if I were his biggest fan.

I said, "Hey, how are you doing? I've always wanted to meet you!"

The boy, his mouth slightly open, stared. He looked confused but excited. He smiled, probably because he couldn't manage to actually say anything.

I poured it on and asked for his autograph.

We found a pen and a couple of pieces of paper and the boy started writing, spending several seconds on each letter. His mother smiled. I don't think she knew who I was, but she seemed to be touched by the gentle attention I gave her son. The boy finished, smiled, and started to walk away.

Then I asked, "Do you think you'd like my autograph?"

But the more successful I became, the more I had to deal with (or try to avoid) the media, and the more autographs I was being asked to sign. For a while, I'd sign them and include a Bible verse. But eventually I got to the point where I would try not to sign any, opting for a photograph or even a handshake.

I've learned to enjoy my freedom and at times, my anonymity. When I'm out in public invariably, someone will walk up and say that I look like Barry Sanders, often adding "but you're too small to be him."

Fame changed every relationship I'd ever had, except the one with my mother. Everyone changed. At times, it was frustrating. Other times, it was maddening. Most of the time, it was just lonely.

I ALWAYS FOUND DEALING WITH PEOPLE TO BE THE MOST DIFFICULT TASK I HAD AS A PLAYER.

The boy smiled again, slightly embarrassed. I gave him my autograph and he walked away grinning and looking up at his mother. I don't think he ever managed to say a word except maybe a thank you.

It's funny, but as naturally as that exchange came for me, and with all of the time I spent in front of cameras and microphones, I always found dealing with people to be the most difficult task I had as a player. I was uncomfortable signing autographs. When someone approaches, I feel as if I'm suddenly the center of attention. I appreciate the fans and feel grateful that they're interested in me, but when I'm out with my family or friends it's hard to shift roles, to be an average person one minute and in the spotlight the next.

I was one of a handful of notable athletes with a squeaky-clean image. The problem with such images is that they are static. They don't allow for growth or maturity. Growing up in Kansas and going to college in Oklahoma, I entered the league about as green and as earnest as a young man could be. On campus, when people would ask where I planned to go when I finished there, I told them "I want to go to heaven."

In the league, I had to grow up quickly, and I found out quickly that players on the field were warriors, but off the field we were the prey of everyday scammers and hustlers. After just a year of dealing with them, I longed to face the fire-breathing linemen and linebackers on the football field

1989	1,470
1990	1,304
1991	1,548
1992	1,352
1993	1,115
1994	1,883
1995	

2053

At the height of my career, I received much more attention from fans and the media than I expected.

who wanted to tear my head off. At least they honor certain rules and boundaries. At least they don't follow you home. At least they don't ring your phone incessantly.

Despite the fact that my wife and my best friend are journalists, their world of words and images remains a mystery to me. When I came into the league, I did interviews sparingly, not knowing that when it comes to the media, you can run but you can't hide. I'm the type of player who does his talking on the field, not in the locker room. I deliver my message through the way I play, and I assumed that approach would be enough for people. I hadn't learned yet that when you're quiet, you forfeit your right to fairness and self-definition. If you don't talk, the media will talk for you. Then again, if I knew that, I may have talked even less.

I always had a cordial but uneasy relationship with the media.

I'm no expert, but I think people in the media create these caricatures for a couple of reasons.

First, subjects and sources have to fit neatly into stereotypes for easy packaging, so I became the "Aw shucks, Midwestern Bible boy," someone easy for readers/viewers to recognize in the brief moments reporters have to hook them.

Second, it is also easier to do superficial stories than to do the intense reporting necessary to find out what really makes people tick, what experiences have broken their hearts, and what inspires them. You have to get close to them and talk to them, and at the same time, you have to give a little bit of yourself in the process.

That kind of intense reporting doesn't happen very much, and I'll admit to not trusting people enough to let it happen.

THE HUNT AND THE HUNTED

After we've been reduced to mere caricatures—no longer people with lives and emotions and loved ones—the hunt escalates. I can recall trying to enjoy a night with my wife not long after I announced my retirement. Our evening was interrupted when glaring lights and probing cameras showed up outside the venue. Some nut had started what amounted to a "Find Barry" contest. If you saw me (and their cameras always spotted me eventually) then you won fifty dollars. This contest apparently was meant to hound me back onto the team.

Antics such as that contest caused me to be reluctant to go out in public. After announcing my retirement I just didn't want to deal with the fall-out among the media and the fans. So I headed for London. But while the plane was still sitting on the tarmac hoards of journalists, moving like groaning zombies, were trying to board. I can't tell you how concerned I was as we sat there and how relieved I was when the stewardesses finally closed the doors.

I've always wondered how journalists would feel if athletes could somehow find a way to rate them day in and day out, hound them in their personal lives, and even call for their firing or removal. What if we kept track of all of the corrections and typos and grammar busts that creep into their copy? I can only hope that someday we'll find a way. I may sound bitter, but I'm really not. As I said, some of my best friends are journalists.

After some time away from the spotlight, I've been able to put all of this attention in perspective. I remember HBO inviting me to a televised fight held in Detroit's Joe Louis arena. I told them that I couldn't make it, but for some reason my response didn't get to the announcers. They announced to the crowd that I was there.

People booed my name with the enthusiasm that they used to cheer for me from the stands. It was disappointing, but I also looked at it sort of as a compliment. I felt as though they still wanted to see me play. They weren't happy that I retired. They wanted me back on the field, and the booing was a window into their disappointment.

People enjoyed what I did, and I'm at peace with that.

10

SPLENDOR ON THE GRASS

Anyone who has ever done anything astounding started out with a vision of what he or she wanted to create. That vision begins with a picture you play over and over in your mind. For me, the vision formed on fall Saturday afternoons while watching Tony Dorsett, the University of Pittsburgh's amazing running back, pierce the line and rocket down the sideline. It formed on Sunday afternoons when I saw Marcus Allen gliding like a figure skater over the turf.

After watching them, I would run outside and re-create the scenes in the front yard, imagining myself making the moves and running the way I'd seen those great players do it. I would create the vision as precisely as possible.

BARRY SANDERS

Take the pitch and tuck the ball tightly in the crook of your arm. Float to the right, following the blockers. Eyes up. Control your speed, then—bam! Punch a hole in the line. Defenders fly at you like snowflakes, but you ski around them, sliding down a green mountainside. More arrive, others follow. You stop and they run past. You plant right, wait for them to run there, and then burst left, their hands snatching air and their facemasks mowing grass.

Suddenly the field opens, and you're alone with the sound of your rhythmic breathing and thudding heartbeat. No crowd, no coaches, no teammates. The bouncing landscape looms larger ahead of you. Your cleats don't seem to be touching the ground. Legs burning, chest on fire. The goal line. A flood of sounds. Cheering. Whistles. Teammates.

For me, running was a spiritual act. *Page 79:* **That's me running as a Lion and** *at left* **as a Cowboy.**

Then I would open my eyes.

It was a dream so real I could almost touch the grass. Taste the sweet air. Feel the texture of the ball. Running the football was something almost spiritual for me. It was the first thing I ever paid close attention to as a kid, the first thing that caught my eye about the game of football. I have always loved basketball, especially dribbling past a defender and dunking or flicking a jumper over someone's outstretched hand. As a kid, I spent hours at recess playing soccer. I used to love to watch Sugar Ray Leonard shower his opponents with shots that landed like steel raindrops. But football always was my favorite sport.

No play in football is like a nice long run. Every facet of the act fascinated me: running through the line; making people miss. I wanted to do it. And I wanted to do it in the way that I'd envisioned. To witness that live, to see it happening before your eyes, is incredible. It took me away to another world. I saw what I wanted to do in Tony D. and O.J. and Marcus Allen. O.J. didn't just run the ball. Marcus didn't just run the ball. They looked graceful. They moved me.

I remember people talking about how NBA-great Larry Bird prepared for games. A couple of hours before tip-off, Larry was already facing the defenders in his mind. He'd lower his shoulder and drive toward the man, pressing him onto his heels, then pull up for the fade away. He'd back his man in, and then spin to the board with a finger-roll. He'd chase a ball out of bounds, leap, snag the ball, and turn in mid-air to fire a shot from behind the backboard that splashed through the net.

During the game, it may have looked like Larry was improvising, especially that behind-the-backboard shot that dropped all net. But those are things he had practiced or at least thought about or that he had prepared himself to do. It was the first time the scrambling defender had seen the scenario, but Larry had replayed those scenes in his mind over and over. You've got to have such a vision.

I had a vision, too, and it was beautiful. I put everything I was into it. Loving it dragged me into the weight room to lift weights until my arms burned, and it dragged me to run steep mountain slopes during the off-season until my lungs crackled. It made me prepare. It made me dream about what I might do next.

HOW (NOT) TO CARRY THE FOOTBALL

Football is about forward progress. You get three chances to move the ball ten yards through a human wall dug in to stop you. If you don't make it in those three chances, you kick the ball away from the goal you're defending, and your opponent then tries to run through your human wall. Walls collide again and again in the fight for yardage. As the team plows forward—north and south, straight ahead—every inch counts. You keep your legs driving.

Moving backward is anathema. In fact, teams are penalized for infractions by being moved away from their goal. Yardage, football's currency, gets swapped on every play. Stopping, jumping, moving from side to side, and especially reversing field and running backward, gives that wall of defenders time to fight through your wall and mob you for a loss. You lose yardage. Runners are taught from their infancy to avoid these temptations. But laws are made to be broken, and I broke virtually all of the rules of carrying the ball.

On any given play, I'd stop my feet. I'd jump. I'd dance side to side in the narrow paths that form between those two crashing walls. I'd sometimes run backward. Angelo Dundee, Muhammad Ali's legendary trainer, once said that the champ "did everything wrong, but it turned out right." People have said that I did everything wrong, but it turned out right—sometimes.

I would often lose ground with the chances I took by stopping, spinning, jumping, and reversing field. But I was adhering to a much more important rule. A long time ago, Daddy told me to run like a scared rabbit, so that's what I did. I figured the only rule that mattered was the one that said Don't Get Tackled.

Perhaps my favorite such run came when I was a freshman in college in a game against Houston. It wasn't a long run—something like 11 yards. I didn't even score. But it was special. I just remember dancing around in the backfield and changing directions. I remember guys falling around me, and it was almost like I was controlling them, controlling their movements.

As a player, I lived for the compressed excitement of those moments, the moments when people stand up and stop breathing as they watch. They aren't cheering yet, but the anticipation, the possibility, pulls them to

Barry and I were roommates with the Playboy All-American team in 1988, and we got to know each other, but I only got a chance to play against him once. The game was in Detroit in 1991. As we prepared for the Lions, our plan was to get as many guys around Barry Sanders as possible and try to get a good tackle on him. That was tough to do. You rarely saw anybody really get a shot on him, helmet to helmet.

When you're trying to stop him, you surround him, you try to contain him. You're also trying not to make the ESPN highlights with him faking you out of your shoes. I remember on one play they threw a flare pass to the side of the field, and I came running up on him. I got about five yards away and just stopped, waiting to see what he was going to do. I wasn't about to let him make me look like a fool. I wasn't going to make "Sports Center" that night, with Chris Berman making funny remarks about me. When you're trying to tackle Barry Sanders, there's a very high probability that this will happen to you.

At the end of the game, I was relieved to be done with it. We lost 17-13, but I'd made thirteen tackles and didn't get made to look stupid by Barry. We did a pretty good job of keeping him surrounded, but he still hit us for over a hundred yards.

As far as guys who were tough to tackle, I'd put him right at the top. A big back might be tough to bring down, but you can get a hit on him. He'll let you make contact. But tackling Barry was like tackling a slippery eel in the ocean.

Louis Oliver, Former Miami Dolphins Safety

DADDY TOLD ME TO RUN LIKE A SCARED RABBIT, SO THAT'S WHAT I DID.

their feet. It's the same kind of startled excitement you feel for a split second when you catch yourself falling over backward in a chair. I wanted to exist within those moments, play in those moments, ignite those moments.

I don't think I could have been as successful a runner if I had followed the rules and plunged right into the chests of bigger, stronger defenders. That approach only would have made it easier for them to catch me.

Before the start of training camp one year, the coaches showed the team a highlight tape of the history of the franchise. The tape included a 13-yard touchdown run I made against Green Bay in 1994. I started right, doubled back to the left, stopped, and cut back three more times. Nine of the eleven Packer defenders hit me during the run—pad-on-pad shots that could have resulted in tackles—but none of them brought me down. The Packers had many excellent players, and I was fortunate to elude them. Touchdown.

It's possible to make a lot of people miss with this running style. The longer you're on your feet, the better your chance at scoring. One run against Chicago was a prime example. It was just an off-tackle play to the right. I remember thinking that this would be

an average run, a couple of yards, if that far. But then, I remember running into defenders, and we kind of bounced outside. I remember that they started falling down and that I was kind of surprised that I wasn't going down with them. It is weird trying to describe it, but usually, it's almost like you know when you're going to get tackled and when you're not going to get tackled. That play was a time when I had that surprised feeling. I thought, okay, I'm not down yet. I braced myself, and then I remember being able to break free and run to the goal.

Former Bears linebacker Brian Cox said that I once made him miss four tackles in a single play—a great tribute from a great player. Former Packer and Eagle defensive end Reggie White said I was the only player he ever feared physically. "There was one guy since I've been playing that I was afraid of because he could beat us at any moment. That was Barry." I admired Reggie both as a player and as a person, so his respect for my running skills meant a lot to me.

I played against some great defenders and some great defensive coaches, including linebacker Lawrence Taylor of the New York Giants, and Tony Dungy, when he was the defensive coordinator for the Minnesota

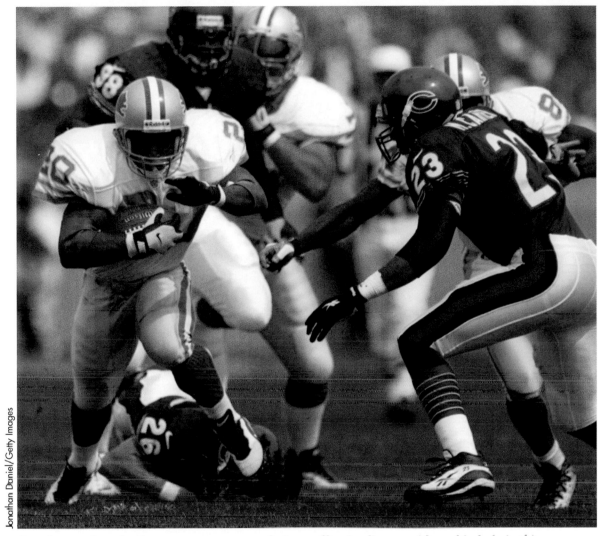

Jonathan Daniel/Getty Images

Running against the Bears was never easy, but my offensive line provides a big hole in this game, played in Chicago in September of 1997. We won, 32-7.

NOW YOU SEE HIM

Vikings and later the head coach for the Tampa Bay Buccaneers. These players and coaches— more on them in the next chapters—slowed me down, and sometimes they stopped me. I'll have to ask them how they did it. Taylor once told me after a game that he was relieved to see that we weren't running out of an I-formation. If we had used that formation, he said, they wouldn't have been able to stop me.

I remember thinking, "Wow. What a compliment." It was my first-ever start as a Detroit Lion.

Looking back on my career, I'm grateful for God's gift to me. I loved to run, and I feel blessed that I was able to spend many years doing it. When a vision becomes a reality, it's a great feeling.

11

R I V A L S

Something about the word "rivalry" bothers me. It seems to imply jealousy or dislike. It never was like that with me and the people I played against. Though we were rivals, I guess, in the traditional sense of the word, I didn't see them as enemies or feel negative emotions toward them. And I had a unique perspective, because every defender on the other team was keying on me.

During one game, when word got out that I had a sore ankle, I can remember guys in the post-play scrum trying to twist my ankle. If the turf under the piles of players on top of me could talk, it could tell you things that wouldn't get past a censor. You certainly couldn't print what was said. One of the more tame comments was something like, "Not today! Not today!" By that phrase they meant that I wouldn't be making any spectacular runs against their defense that day. I never said anything back. I'd smile, nod,

and trot back to the huddle, and then I'd come flying back hard on the next play. If I accomplished my goal, I really didn't need to say anything, did I?

But I didn't dislike anyone. I have to admit I enjoyed the trash talk. It made the games more fun, more challenging. The talk often brought out the best in me, and I knew it never was personal. When the game ended, that type of talk stopped.

One "rival" running back who I like a lot is Emmitt Smith. He's always been very complimentary to me and is just a genuine, authentic person. Though we played in the league together for years, I didn't realize until later that he was such a fun-loving guy around his teammates. He's a lot more outgoing than I thought. When he asked me to join his Run for the Record campaign in 2002, I was excited to be a part of it.

Though Emmitt is a great guy, we did compete. Before one of the Pro Bowls, for example, the two of us disappeared for a friendly competition—nothing serious, just fun-and-games type of stuff. We were throwing the ball with either hand, running and juking, stuff like that. We were trying to out-do each other, but I can't say if we declared a winner. Since he now holds the rushing record, I'll say that he won.

Neal Anderson was another back I really admired. At the beginning of my career, whenever I'd go into a contract negotiation, I would always hear some reference to "Neal Anderson-type money." Whenever we played the Bears, there always was a little bit of competition among the backs—who could pull off the best runs, who could gain the most yards, things like that. Anderson was a great rival in

Page 87: **The Vikings were a particularly tough defense to run against. That's me getting clobbered by linebacker Dixon Edwards.**

that way. I've always felt he was a very underrated player. He made plenty of long, spectacular runs, and he had game-breaking speed that a lot of fans don't always associate with him. People didn't know that he was so fast.

I enjoyed those types of rivalries, and I enjoyed them even more on certain fields. Games took on a special significance because of the stadium's place in football lore and because of the current players still carrying the team's banner of excellence. Playing at Green Bay against Brett Favre was a treat in that way. Favre was a great player who brought an extra bit of energy to the game. Playing against Troy Aikman, Joe Montana, and Steve Young were special moments too. I recognized that we were competing, but I couldn't help but be a fan and witness with the rest of the crowd just why these men were so special. It was great being on the same field with them.

TOUGH DEFENDERS

I could only compare numbers with my fellow running backs in the league, but I had to go head-to-head against my defensive rivals. John Lynch, the safety for the Tampa Bay Buccaneers, was one of those guys. I wanted him accounted for on blocking assignments. I always wanted to know where he was. The same is true for Brian Cox of the Chicago Bears. He was going to take his shot no matter what. He'd say, "Forget what I've been practicing all week. I'm going to take my shot and whatever happens, happens."

Stephen Dunn/Getty Images

Emmitt eludes Tommy Bennett of the Arizona Cardinals during a game at Texas Stadium in September of 1998.

I guess you could say Barry and I were rivals in that we were always very conscious of each other. When I'd watch ESPN after a game, I always wanted see what B. Sanders had done that day. For me, it was one of those things where I had to know what he was doing. And I knew that if anybody had a chance to have a breakout game any week, it was Barry.

When I first met him, I was in awe, because I'd seen him run in college and saw what he could do, and then I saw what he could do in the NFL. I thought, "This guy here's the best." I knew that if he was the best, I would have to do everything in my power to achieve his level and pass it, if I was going to make myself the best.

His ability to stop, restart, and change direction, all within a five-yard radius, is better than anybody I ever saw. His hips were amazing. It looked like he almost could turn them completely around his back. And he had great balance, great leg strength, and great speed. He was fast. Some people underestimate his speed, saying he was more quick than fast.

I can't think of any runner who compares to him. People often bring up Gale Sayers, but I've watched Sayers, and he didn't do any of the things that you saw Barry do. Sayers had speed and agility, no question, but he never did the things that Barry did every time you watched him. I've never seen anybody who had the abilities Barry possessed.

One of those abilities, and one you don't hear a lot of people talk about, was his ability to avoid the big hit. Guys couldn't get a good hit on him, which was important, because that kept him healthy and in the game. Some people criticized him, saying he was flashy but that too many times he'd lose two or three yards because of his running style. But he never had an All-Pro offensive line in front of him, opening up holes. He lost yards sometimes because he was too busy trying to make five guys miss.

At the same time, I don't get into those discussions about what he could have done if he had played on a better team. You just don't know. It might have helped him to have a better surrounding cast, but then you have to wonder if he would have gotten as many touches as he got. Maybe he would, and maybe he wouldn't. Everybody's got an opinion. I think it's better to focus on and remember what he *did* do than get into all of that speculation.

As for being rivals, I'll say that when the Cowboys played the Lions, I was intent on watching what he was doing, and I wanted to have a better day than he did. I would appreciate his runs and admire what he was doing, but as an individual, when you're playing against one of the best, you want to dominate, so that you can show that you're one of the best, too.

But the only time I ever would root against him was when we were playing against him. Barry is a prince of a guy. He's quiet and very reserved, at least until you get to know him. He's an all-around good person, and so when we weren't playing against him, I was rooting for him to do well. I was with him.

Emmitt Smith, NFL All-Time Leading Rusher

NOW YOU SEE HIM

BARRY SANDERS

I'm running away from Bears linebacker Mike Singletary, who always treated me like a kid brother—except during games.

The biggest thing about playing against Barry was that you knew it wasn't over till it was over. That rule applied to games as well as to individual plays. There was a play that I remember when we thought we had him—seven or eight guys right there on him, and the next thing I knew he was running down the field for a touchdown.

I've never seen anyone, or played against anyone, who was like him. He defied all the rules of tackling. Even if you did everything you're supposed to do—got your feet right, looked at his belly button, positioned yourself, wrapped him up—he still would run past you. He had great vision and great feet. And he had the ability to always move those feet, even when you had him wrapped up. If you didn't get his feet, you weren't going to get him.

To have success against him you had to be a disciplined defense, and you had to have perfect technique. You couldn't just lunge at him. If you were able to get him running east to west, you had a chance. If he was moving north-south, forget about it. He was going to get you.

I guess I played against him maybe eight times. The first time we played against him was his rookie year. We had heard about him and watched some film of him, and we said, "This kid has been making other teams look silly. Let's show him how the Bears play defense." Then he gained something like 120 yards against us. We couldn't believe it. Nobody did that to the Bears. After that first game, I knew the kid was special. It wasn't just a matter of being a good back or having a good game. This kid was special.

The Lions were in our division so we saw a lot of him. If he wasn't going to play for some reason, we were more at ease against them. In a lot of ways, Barry *was* that team, and I say that with no disrespect to the other guys. They'll understand what I'm saying. When he was there, they played differently. They walked onto the field differently. The coaches coached differently.

Even if he beat you or made you look bad, you couldn't get mad at him. He was such a class kid, such a gentleman. When he scored, he didn't slam the ball down. He didn't tell guys that he had made them look bad. And he could have done that, because he sure had plenty of chances to do it. But Barry was a quality person with a lot of character, and he didn't feel the need to prove anything to anybody or show-up anybody. He would just go about his business. That was Barry.

Mike Singletary, Former Chicago Bears Linebacker

NOW YOU SEE HIM

John and Brian weren't the only ones. There were other players, too, who might be called rivals—guys I wanted to avoid. But if I had a rivalry with a defensive unit, it had to be the Minnesota Vikings. Whenever we played the Vikings, there was always some competition. They had great hitters, such as Joey Browner. He would have made a good Raider. Back in the early '90s, they had a great defense—one of those unique defenses that don't come around often. They had Browner, Chris Doleman, Keith Millard, and Henry Thomas. How do you get all those guys on the same team?

And they had a genius for a defensive coordinator—Tony Dungy, who now is the head coach for the Indianapolis Colts. I faced Tony with the Vikings, then later with Tampa Bay. Tony always had his teams ready to play, especially the defense. I looked forward to the

BARRY SANDERS

Brian Bahr/Getty Images

Coach Bill Parcells always prepared his teams well. He gave them something extra. That's quarterback Vinnie Testaverde standing next to him.

challenges he'd lay out for us. I'm sure that other teams studied what Dungy and those guys were doing to bottle me up, but not everyone could do it. Other teams didn't have the personnel to do what the Vikings were doing. The success they had in stopping me is a testament to the their defense.

Some of those other teams weren't above some creative preparation of their own. I saw a videotape in which one team's assistant coach said that the staff actually bought a chicken to use in their scout offense to simulate my herky-jerky running style. I'm not sure it worked, though, because apparently they couldn't get the lazy chicken to run.

Another coach I admired a lot was Bill Parcells, who I faced with several teams, including the New York Jets. You could see at field level just how much he raised the level of play. You could tell that his players were equipped with something extra. When you lined up against a Parcells team, you almost felt as if you were not only facing inspired players, but the coach as well, because his influence extended from sideline to sideline and from end zone to end zone.

Though I mentioned some defensive players who I wanted to avoid on the field, let me also say that some of those guys were the nicest people off the field. I especially liked, as well as admired, Reggie White and Mike Singletary. During the game, I was always conscious of them. We all played in the same division so I lined up against them often, and they were truly the best I played against. After the game, Mike would always come up to me and tell me to take care of myself, to be careful, almost like a big brother. He seemed genuinely concerned.

I spent more time off the field with Reggie. I don't want to say he was a gentle giant, but he was a very pleasant and good person. He wanted the best for me off the field and tried to steer me around the pitfalls of making bad choices where friends were concerned. He took an interest in my personal life and made sure I had good people around me. He just reached out as a friend. It always was so interesting to see a guy who manhandled 300-pound linemen but who also had such a gentle spirit. On the field, you'd better be ready to compete against Reggie. Off the the field, it's hard to imagine feeling that he was a rival.

Brian Bahr/Getty Images

NOW YOU SEE HIM

Packers lineman Reggie White squashes Shannon Sharpe of the Denver Broncos.

12

COACHES

One of my first coaches was one of my favorites, a man named William McNeal. He was my eighth-grade coach for the Wichita Colts, a Little League team. He helped me believe in myself with his encouraging attitude.

He didn't play favorites, and he paid as much attention to the weakest players as he did to the strongest. It wasn't one of those situations where if you weren't as big or as fast as other kids on the team he'd forget about you. His confidence in us made us all better players. He was great with kids. He was jovial and just out there to have a good time.

I had a different experience with another of my coaches, as I mentioned earlier. My ninth-grade year was really the first one I can remember not being a factor on the team. I wasn't a factor at all. I hardly ever played. As I said before, the coach and Daddy got into it about that, too.

Jonathan Daniel/Getty Images

Previous page: **Coach Wayne Fontes who led the Lions throughout most of my career. A fun-loving guy off the field, Wayne was all business during games.** *At left:* **That's Pat Jones, my coach at OSU. He did a great job of preparing me for pro ball.**

BARRY SANDERS

Daddy was disappointed about my lack of playing time.

In a previous chapter I mentioned Dale Burkholder, my coach during my senior year in high school. He may have been one of the most influential people in my life outside my family. He might be my favorite coach in all the years I played. Coach B, who now is an assistant principal in Topeka, is the type of coach I'd want for my son. He enjoyed his job as much as any coach I'd ever seen. He loved being around kids. We weren't a burden. He wasn't playing games with our heads or telling us that he was going to do one thing and then do something else. We trusted him.

If he disliked anyone, he didn't show it. It was fun for everyone. Everyone liked Coach B. I've heard stories about how he put his job on the line when he finally started me at tailback, over the objections of the athletic director, Bob Shepler, who as I discussed earlier was the previous head coach. I don't

have much to say about him. I'm not certain why he made the decisions he made.

Beyond our high school friendship, Coach B really lobbied for me as a player to college recruiters and pestered the local media with my highlight tape to spread the word about me. These were things I could never do for myself. I might never have made it to Oklahoma State to play for Pat Jones if not for Coach B's help and lobbying.

Pat treated me fairly. He was a no-nonsense coach who brought the most out of his players. He was a good motivator. During my years at OSU, I learned a lot from him. Most of all, he taught me the academic side of football, the mental preparation and the study that players have to do before a game. I learned how to analyze defenses, looking for patterns and tendencies while watching film of the upcoming opponent. By the time I declared for the draft, I was ready to play in the NFL. Pat had prepared me to be a good pro during my years playing for him.

COACHES IN THE NFL

After playing for Pat Jones, Wayne Fontes marked another change in direction. He had been the interim coach in 1988, taking over the team after the previous head coach, Darryl Rogers, was fired. My first year in the league was his first full year as a head coach. At the beginning, he probably listened to too many in people and too many different ideas.

Considering how the Lions sort of plugged him in as a stop-gap, many of us wondered in that first year how much faith and confidence the organization actually had in him. Despite that situation, I think he developed into a good coach. The guys liked him. I always liked him. We always understood that football was a business and that we were in the business of winning games, but he understood also that there was a time for fun, too. He liked to laugh, and he loved to have a good time. He wasn't so serious that he couldn't laugh with players or even at himself. He also tried to put his players first. He realized that he needed the players as much as the players needed him.

With Wayne, players liked being there: in the locker room and on the field. When he was fired after the '96 season, after we finished 5-11, I was disappointed. I thought he deserved another chance. We'd been to the playoffs almost every other year

AP Photo/Richard Sheinwald

Coach Fontes shows me around the Lions locker room before the start of my rookie season.

BARRY SANDERS

When I was coaching Barry, players said I treated him a little special. I remember one year at training camp, a veteran receiver stood up and told the rookies, "Coach has probably told you he treats everybody the same. Well, you see that little guy wearing number twenty? Coach treats him different. Don't you ever knock him down."

Everybody had a good laugh, but the player was right. I even had a no-contact rule in practice for Barry. Usually that rule was only for the quarterbacks. The defensive guys like Jerry Ball and Chris Spielman would joke around and say they were going to rush in and crush Barry, but when the play was run, a hole would open up a mile wide.

That's how much they respected him. Every player on that team loved him. They knew he didn't need to prove anything in practice. When the game started, Barry would be ready.

He would make sure he was ready. After a long practice, when the players headed for the locker room, Barry would go down to the end of the field by himself and run sprints. Sometimes he was still at it when the other guys had showered, gotten dressed, and were headed home. They'd stop and watch him. He was amazing, and they knew it. In practice and on the field, he was a no-nonsense player. Everything was a hundred percent.

He was a great runner because he was so well prepared, but he also had great instincts. He had a vision on the field that few people have—knowing when a hole was opening up, seeing something downfield that nobody else saw. It's like he had a sixth sense.

Before games, the players would do different things— listen to music or pound their pads against the wall. Spielman would always walk around in the shower. Barry would lie down with a towel over his head. I'd go around to each of them and shake hands, and when I came to Barry, he'd lift his hand without taking the towel away. He always could sense that I was there.

Wayne Fontes Detroit Record				
Year	Regular Season		Playoffs	
	W	L	W	L
1988	2	3	0	0
1989	7	9	0	0
1990	6	10	0	0
1991	12	4	1	1
1992	5	11	0	0
1993	10	6	0	1
1994	9	7	0	0
1995	10	6	0	0
1996	5	11	0	0
TOTALS	66	67	1	2

He was also one of the nicest people I've ever come across in coaching. As great a runner as he was, he was an even better person. He was an unselfish guy. He didn't care if he touched the ball four times or twenty, if the team was winning, and he always acknowledged the blocking of his teammates. If you had a daughter, you'd say this is the perfect guy for her. I remember liking him the first time I met him, and that feeling never changed. I treated him different because he was special. He made my eight years in Detroit very memorable.

Wayne Fontes, Head Coach, Detroit Lions

with Wayne as our coach. We'd gotten close to a Super Bowl appearance with him.

When the Lions fired Wayne, they hired Bobby Ross, a hard-working, hard-charging coach who was a solid leader. He was demanding and extremely well organized. Our training schedules were so painstakingly arranged that we knew what we were going to do almost by the minute. Many players believed that management

Otto Greule Jr/Getty Images

Bobby Ross, who coached the Lions my last two years in the league, seemed to have very little fun in football, which was a big change from Wayne Fontes.

NOW YOU SEE HIM

had brought in Coach Ross to shape up the team, perhaps blaming Wayne's final losing season on his personable style. Wayne was seen as a player's coach, and the Lions wanted a new approach.

Coach Ross put in long hours. He would arrive around five in the morning and work until ten or eleven at night. Because I played for him for only two years, I didn't get to know him well. I did think, however, that he made some poor personnel decisions, though it's impossible to know if the decisions were made by him or by Chuck Schmidt.

He had a few quirks, too. For example, he didn't like guys on our team helping up guys on the other team. I didn't understand that attitude, which struck as old-fashioned. What difference does it make to show a little sportsmanship? But he knew a lot about the game, and he demanded and deserved respect. From a personal standpoint, I benefited from his emphasis on the running game. Coach Ross gave me the ball, and that philosophy allowed me to gain over 2,000 yards in a season.

13

2 0 5 3

With so many regular-season games, the 1,000-yard season for a running back isn't the standard of success it used to be when a season was only twelve or fourteen games long. Average 62.5 yards over sixteen weeks and you're there.

In 1998, with two games left in the season, thirteen players already had gained 1,000 yards, and six others were poised to reach the mark. At the time, there'd never been sixteen players with 1,000-yard seasons. It seems to me that 1,200 or 1,400 yards is more of a standard. In 1985, nine players had 1,200 or more yards: Marcus Allen, Gerald Riggs, Walter Payton, Joe Morris, Freeman McNeil, Tony Dorsett, James Wilder, Eric Dickerson and Craig James.

I was fortunate enough during my career to average nearly 1,500 yards a season, but until I had a season in

The 215 yards I gained against Tampa Bay on October 12 proved to be a turning point in my run for 2,000.

Barry was never into records and titles, but the year he gained over 2,000 yards was special. We knew he'd be near the top of the league, like he always was, but nobody thought he'd get to 2,000, especially after the first two games, when he had only 53 yards. We were still learning a new offensive system, so the slow start wasn't his fault. And when you look at it, he gained 2,000 yards in fourteen games.

As the season went on and he kept getting 100-yard games, the linemen knew he had a chance at 2,000, but we never discussed it with him. The linemen always went out on Thursday night, and with three games left in the season, we sat together and figured out what he would have to average to get 2,000. We decided to try to help him get what he needed. We had so much respect for him.

You knew on any given play he could go all the way, and that made you give a little extra. I remember one play during that year, in a game against Green Bay. It was third and eighteen, and the coach called a counter-play—a run. In the huddle we were thinking, "Why aren't we passing?" We could have doubted the play call and not given a full effort, but with Barry in the game there was always a chance. So we gave it everything, and Barry broke off a big run and scored a touchdown.

For personal reasons, I'll always remember the last run. He'd gotten the 2,000 yards late in the game on a short run, maybe two yards. Then, near the end of the game, he broke off a 53-yarder. I told him thanks for going out of bounds when he did, because he ended up with 2,053 for the year. His number was 20 and mine was 53, and that was the last game we'd ever play together as teammates. I'll never forget it.

Kevin Glover, Teammate, Detroit Lions

which I got close to 2,000 yards, I didn't think that milestone was possible for me. In 1994, I was seventeen yards shy of 1,900. At the time, only two running backs had passed the 2,000-yard threshold: Dickerson, with 2,105 in 1984; O.J. Simpson, with 2,003 in 1973.

At the beginning of 1997, the season I finally cracked the 2,000-yard mark, it didn't appear as if I'd be joining them. I felt good. I felt strong. But after two games, I had only 53 yards, and reporters started reminding me that I was twenty-nine. In other words, I was getting old.

But I felt like 2,000 was a possibility. I'd run for 1,800 before. I knew that reaching 2,000 depended to some extent on what was going on with the team, but I felt that if I stayed healthy and in the right situation, it was possible. In those first games, against Atlanta and Tampa Bay, I didn't get a lot of carries. Also, in the game against the Buccaneers I had 102 receiving yards and even scored a touchdown, so I felt like I was producing. I didn't feel old. I was ready and able to have a good year. I made myself the player I was because I always wanted to see what I could do next. I wanted to see if I could reach the next level.

Putting my own feelings and goals aside, I had guys blocking for me who really wanted me to get the milestone. I pushed for it as much for them as for myself. After those first two games in '97, however, the goal might have seemed to be a little out of reach. Then things changed. The yards piled up so quickly that my success surprised even me. It had been an up-and-down season for the team, but I was having my best year in years. One game, at Tampa Bay, I had two runs longer than 80 yards and finished with 215 yards on the day.

I can't say that I expected to do it. In the game of pro football, you just never know. Everything has to line up right for you to be able to accomplish something like that. That day in Tampa—October 12— was just such a day, despite the warm Florida weather. Coming there from Detroit, we were thinking about a whole other set of problems, such as cramping up, losing water, fading out because of the heat.

After the first long run, I remember thinking, "Okay, you got the one 80-yard run, and the D is going to be pretty tight the rest of the game." And so when the second one came, I was shocked. In fact, while I was running, I was assuming either I was going to get tired and burn out and somebody was going to catch me, or I wasn't going to make it.

REACHING 2,000

We rode the momentum of the win at Tampa Bay all the way till the last game of the season. Going into that game at home against the New York Jets, I needed more than 130 yards to reach 2,000 yards, and the team needed this win to earn a playoff berth. The pressure was intense, but I found myself enjoying it, energized by the challenge. I felt renewed.

Reaching 2,000 was probably the first individual performance record that I really, really wanted. The Heisman, though I enjoyed the honor of receiving it, just didn't seem real. At the time, I didn't see myself as being in the same league with others who'd won the award. From high school to the pros, as I mentioned earlier, I was content to sit out of the ends of games that my team had won, even when I was just a few yards short of rushing titles. Building up yardage against a beaten opponent for your own personal gain just never seemed respectful or dignified to me.

This time, however, was different. I wanted that 2,000. As we prepared to play

The 1997 Season

WEEK/OPPONENT	RUSHES	YARDS	TOUCHDOWNS
1 ATLANTA	15	33	0
2 TAMPA BAY	10	20	1
3 CHICAGO	19	161	0
4 NEW ORLEANS	18	133	1
5 GREEN BAY	28	139	0
6 BUFFALO	25	107	0
7 TAMPA BAY	24	215	3
8 NY GIANTS	24	105	1
9 GREEN BAY	23	105	0
10 WASHINGTON	15	105	1
11 MINNESOTA	19	108	0
12 INDIANAPOLIS	24	216	2
13 CHICAGO	19	167	3
14 MIAMI	30	137	1
15 MINNESOTA	19	138	0
16 NY JETS	23	184	1
TOTALS	**335**	**2053**	**14**

the Jets, the whole country seemed to be watching to see if I could get it. I even got a telegram from O.J. before the game wishing me luck. I had twenty to thirty family members and friends watching the game from my home and a dozen more in the stands.

The game tested our resolve and the crowd's nerves. We fell behind a Jets team that had a pretty good scheme for stopping us. I'd read that a few years before the game, Coach Bill Parcells had stolen a Super Bowl for his team at the time, the New York Giants, by shortening the game against the offensively superior Buffalo

Hulton Archive/2003 Getty Images

My father revered the great Jim Brown, who still holds the yards-per-carry record for one season.

Bills. On this day in the Silverdome, he seemed to be doing the same thing. He ran short plays that ate up the clock and kept the ball out of our offense's hands and out of my hands, too.

His strategy worked for a while. The Jets scored ten points in the first twelve minutes. At that stage of the game, I only had eight carries and 20 yards. The crowd and my teammates were getting antsy. It wasn't until the third quarter that I really became a factor. On a third and three from our 36 yard line, Scott Mitchell handed me the ball, and I sliced through the line for a 47-yard run.

On the next play, I shot off our left tackle and was in the end zone 15 yards later. We took the lead and never looked back. That 15-yard run turned out to be the winning touchdown. I finished the game with 184 yards, and I finished the season with 2,053. Only Jim Brown finished with a higher yards-per-carry average in a given season. He finished with 6.4 yards per carry in 1963, and I finished with 6.1 yards per carry in 1997.

Interestingly, after the game, Daddy whispered to my friend Mark that I was as good, if not better, than Jim Brown. Daddy had always made a big deal of saying that Jim Brown wasn't just better than me, he was a man among boys. But Daddy, of all people, told Mark that he didn't want to sound vain bragging on his own son. He's never told me that he thought I was better. He just told Mark, as far as I know.

NOW YOU SEE HIM

DOUBTS ABOUT THE FUTURE

I was proud of the accomplishment, but it was tempered by yet another blow. One of my teammates, Reggie Brown, suffered a serious spinal cord injury during the game with the Jets. He had to be given mouth-to-mouth resuscitation on the field. The experience left me thinking more than ever about my professional mortality. As I mentioned in an earlier chapter, my teammate Mike Utley had suffered a similar injury in 1991, and now Reggie was down.

What happened to them truly frightened me. In the back of every player's mind, there is an awareness of the barbaric, dangerous nature of the game. But then, to have that sort of subtle awareness shattered by an event right in front of you sobers you. To see the tragedy and know these people and like them and see how it affects their lives and to be on the field when it happens … I don't know. That's almost enough to make you want to quit right there. That's enough to make you say, how do you go on?

When someone is injured, it lingers. It's always on your mind. It is so eerie. You understand that not only can you get seriously injured but that you actually can die.

I had considered walking away before the season, and Reggie's injury wasn't helping me to stay committed to the game. When I stopped to take an accounting of what I'd done to that point in my career, I realized how much I'd accomplished already. I had league, conference, and team rushing titles, a highlight reel full of electrifying runs, and now membership in the 2,000-yard club and an MVP. Reaching that milestone was something to remember. In the history of the NFL, and despite all the great backs who played before me, only two others had gained more than 2,000 yards. Of course, I give thanks to God for helping me achieve that goal. I also give thanks to my teammates who blocked for me. Without them, I wouldn't have run far at all.

In reaching 2,000, I set another record of fourteen consecutive 100-yard games. No one had ever done that before, and that record means as much to me as any other. Considering the level of competition in the game, I'll always be especially proud of that particular record.

That season gave me pride for a number of reasons. Winning the Most Valuable Player award was a great honor, and by gaining 2,053 yards I jumped from seventh to second on the all-time rushing list. During the year, I had passed Marcus Allen, Franco Harris, Jim Brown, Tony Dorsett, and Eric Dickerson. As I've said, numbers don't mean all that much to me, but being in the company of those great players, especially Jim Brown, meant a great deal to me. Chasing Walter Payton's record, however, never seemed nearly as important to me as it did to a lot of the fans and to the sports media. I had already achieved a level of success that gave me much satisfaction and pride. I didn't need to pass Walter to prove anything more to myself.

A goal that I still hadn't realized, however, was playing in the Super Bowl, and all of the statistical achievements didn't put the team any closer to playing in the big game. The win against the Jets did put us in the playoffs and sent us back to Tampa Bay to

Tom Pidgeon/Getty Images

AP Photo/Bob Broadbeck

Despite the record-setting season, I already was thinking about leaving the game. *Right:* **The serious injury to teammate Reggie Brown added more doubt.** *Next page:* **I face a swarming Buccaneers defense in the playoffs.**

NOW YOU SEE HIM

play in the Wild-Card game. But unlike the day earlier in the season when I made the two 80-yard runs, this time we lost. There were no 80-yard runs for me. Instead, I finished with 65 yards on eighteen carries, and the Bucs beat us 20-10. It was another frustrating end of a season. Though I remained proud of the records, and despite everything I'd been able to accomplish, I was increasingly unsure about my professional future.

AP Photo/Pete Cosgrove

14

RUN FROM THE RECORD

Soon after I reached the 2,000-season mark, the talk around me moved to a new mountain: Walter Payton's career rushing record of 16,726 yards. By the end of the 1998 season, I was only 1,457 yards behind Walter, and I'd been averaging more than 1,500 yards a season, so my setting a new record looked like a sure thing.

People took notice, and I quickly found myself in the middle of "Run for the Record," a licensing and sponsorship campaign put together by Pro Access, a Miami sports-and-entertainment marketing company. The company planned to interest sponsors in using my march to the record to sell cars, cereal, sportswear, and other products. The idea interested me,

I met Barry Sanders for the first time during the early stage of creating Run for the Record. I was sitting with his agent in a trendy Detroit restaurant (jackets required) when he walked in. Barry was provided with a loaner jacket, and then made his way to our table. I've been around a lot of celebrities in my day, but the way the restaurant stood still as he threaded past the tables amazed me. I was even more amazed by how unassuming he was during our conversation and how easy it felt to be around him. Although he was quiet, he had a certain humor and candor that made me feel very comfortable.

When designing the Run for the Record campaign, we positioned Barry as the "American Hero." Since childhood, I believed that a hero is someone who saves the day by doing something extraordinary. I soon came to realize that Barry is a hero for what he doesn't do. Arguably one of the most exciting athletes of this generation, Barry is the anti-celebrity. He generally wants to get to know people. He would rather have an in-depth conversation than sign a napkin or a football for someone. He is genuinely modest. Sometimes I wonder if the thought of all the hoopla about the breaking of Walter's record caused Barry's sudden departure. The record was his, but in classic Barry style, he just politely flipped the ball to Emmitt Smith and walked to the sideline.

Eric Levin, Creator of Run for the Record

Previous page: **My third 80-yard run of 1997 came against the Indianapolis Colts. I ran even harder from the media frenzy surrounding my approach toward breaking Walter Payton's rushing record. That's Walter on the next page.**

BARRY SANDERS

in part because of the charity affiliations involved with it: The United Negro College Fund and the Detroit Youth Foundation. The proposal was exciting, in some ways, but it also thrust me into the middle of a marketing frenzy, which made me uneasy.

I've never shared with anyone exactly how much that record meant to me. I valued it. It represented a real accomplishment and the kind of challenge that kept the blood circulating in my career. The record was a milestone, a career achievement that so many other great backs had never achieved— backs who I admire tremendously. It showed a sustained level of success, and it showed consistency through year after year in a punishing game. For all of those reasons, it was important to me.

However, I never valued it so much

that I thought it was worth my dignity or Walter's dignity to pursue it amid so much media and marketing attention. Only Walter, who at the time was dying from a rare form of liver cancer, seemed to understand how I felt.

"If you have never played the game of football," Walter told reporters, "you can never begin to understand what is going through Barry's heart and mind at this time. It is not about money. It is not about statistics. It is about the romance kindled by playing the game the way it was supposed to be played."

Walter also was quoted as saying that for his own selfish reasons, he wanted to see me continue playing but added, "As I'm engulfed in my personal trials, my family and life are more important than any yard or touchdown ever scored. And in a sense, Barry is fighting for the same." He must have been

inside of my head walking around. I couldn't have said it more eloquently.

The "Run for the Record" campaign exacted a toll from the start. As I discussed in an earlier chapter, I've never been fond of public attention or a lot of dealing with the media. I don't mean to sound aloof; being in the spotlight just isn't in my nature. Not long after the campaign began, I found myself skipping rallies and functions meant to drum up support, spark interest with fans, and attract sponsors. To make matters more complicated, Bobby Ross hated the idea, saying that the campaign would weaken team chemistry by focusing on one player instead of the team. As I said earlier, Bobby was a traditionalist, but he did have a point. I didn't want the focus of the team to be on me. The focus should be on doing whatever it takes to win games.

I wondered if that focus was possible amid all the media and marketing hoopla. Meanwhile, my frustrations with management continued to mount, while my love for the game spilled out of me. One of my agents was growling at Pro Access, demanding to know why he should allow anyone else around his agency's star client. The other agent seemed eager for the campaign to continue.

As if all these complications weren't enough, I rolled my Range Rover, and suddenly the chase was on to find a company that would insure me in case I suffered some sort of career-ending injury before breaking the record.

Eric Levin, the owner of Pro Access, fought through almost all of the obstacles, but he had overlooked an "out" clause that I'd asked him to add to the contract—a clause that allowed for my retirement. He must have assumed no one would retire so close to one of the most sacred records in professional sports. Who would pass on millions of dollars in endorsements? Who would walk out on a $36-million contract? He and a great many others soon found out that I would.

15

I KNEW IT
WAS OVER

I talked about retiring long before actually doing it. Most of the time, jokingly. One time, while stretching with Herman Moore and Tracey Scroggins, I teased that one day while they were all stretching I'd suddenly walk into the locker room and never come back. They thought the idea was hilarious.

But when the end finally came, it wasn't at all funny. I cried, and I'm not certain why. Maybe the tears came pouring out because I had just endured perhaps the most emotionally draining season I'd ever played—a 5-11 season, our second in the past three. We had made the playoffs the previous year, and everyone had expected us to do better.

Maybe I cried because I knew, for the first time since I could remember, I wouldn't be playing football anymore. An all-

consuming part of my life had just died. It felt like losing a close friend, a fulfilling relationship, or a sustaining hopefulness. Or all three. The tears could have come from exhaustion, the kind of fatigue that a marathoner's mind fights off long after his or her body is supposed to have shut down from exertion.

In my last game, we were playing in Baltimore against the Ravens on a raw, rainy afternoon in December of 1998. During my career I rarely fumbled, but I had uncharacteristically let the ball—and the game—slip through my fingers. We lost 19-10.

Also uncharacteristically, the guy who never exploded in celebration when crossing the goal line, the guy who kept his emotions tucked away as tightly as he tucked away the football, cried in front of several teammates in the locker room. The game hadn't been important to either team. Neither was headed for the playoffs. I think a few people saw me crying, but no one said anything. I was crying because I knew it was over.

SHOTS TO THE PSYCHE

I'd considered leaving for years and for no single reason. Around the middle of my career, the game became something else, almost a burden in a lot of ways, and I stopped loving it. My achievements in 1997 came in spite of my waning desire.

Ever watch a boxing match? The fight is rarely decided on one punch. Most fights amount to violent chess matches in which the fighters bank and deposit pain, save and spend their energy. Stingers attack from their toes, circling and circling and flicking jabs against the opponent's face until the accumulation of blows and the loss

of stamina topples the other fighter. Sluggers forge ahead, chewing through leather, swallowing punches just to land a few stabbing body shots that send waves of pain rippling over the opponent's body, the kind of shots that steal your wind and your will.

I think that's what happened to me. I lost my will. I just wasn't willing anymore, and the series of shots I'd taken in the previous seasons siphoned off my commitment. Those shots weren't physical. They weren't collisions during games. Few people actually got hard shots on me in my ten years in the league. I was still in great shape. My ninth year was my best ever. I'm referring more to shots to my psyche. Disappointments. Losses. Betrayals even.

A number of these shots involved the loss of key players, who either were traded away or allowed to go to other teams. We lost Jerry Ball (I used to live on Jerry's wife's cooking), Lomas Brown, Chris Spielman, Bennie Blades, and others. It was difficult to lose All-Pro players and respected teammates, particularly when the problem didn't seem to involve money. The team was signing free agents for more money, and the contract negotiations with these new players seemed to go smoothly. Meanwhile, players who had proven their value to the team were discarded or ignored. When I wanted to restructure my contract, for example, I had to hold out just to get management to the table.

I had thought about leaving even before signing the next-to-the-last contract. The communication gap widened by the week between Lions' management and me, mostly with GM Chuck Schmidt. While I was negotiating a new contract, I received another shot when I was told, "Just because you're the best player on the team doesn't mean you have to be the highest paid."

The comment didn't make me angry, but it did make me think: "Is this team serious about winning?" When I arrived in 1989, we were rebuilding. During the next few years, little by little, attendance started climbing, my jerseys began selling out, and electricity was returning to the Silverdome. And despite holding virtually every Lions rushing record, I continued to push myself. As I mentioned in an earlier chapter, when I was a rookie I'd eat a grocery sack full of Suzy Q's and candy before a game. By the end of my career, I was eating boiled vegetables and keeping myself fit year round.

But by 1998 we were in an awful slide back into rebuilding. After all those years, I'd come full circle. It was tough to stay focused and motivated. Walter Payton was right when he said that if you can't play the way the game was meant to be played, you shouldn't play at all. I knew deep down that my heart wasn't in it anymore. I'd thought about retiring before the 1997 season, when I rushed for over 2,000 yards. I was running on fumes then.

By urging me on toward Walter's career rushing record, everyone was missing an important point: If rushing titles never motivated me before—as evidenced by my pulling myself out of games in high school, college, and in my rookie season—then why would such a record be a motivation to continue playing now?

When I was growing up, sports were everything to me. If I wasn't playing sports, I was thinking about playing, and if I wasn't thinking about it I was dreaming about it. Making it to the pros was the ultimate, and I felt like I had so much to prove from the start. Coming from a small school and being criticized for not playing bigger schools (as if I made the schedules), I wanted to prove that I was good enough to play pro ball, if only to myself.

Given my success in the league, I'd proven that I was good enough, and so that motivation was gone. In the final few years of my career, I only had the team's success to motivate me. I wanted to win. But by those final years, I began to wonder seriously about the motivations of some of the people in the front office. It was hard to guess their bottom line, but it certainly wasn't winning.

TEAMMATES AND WINNING

When they got rid of Kevin Glover, they convinced me that their goal wasn't anywhere close to being about winning games. In 1997, the season before he was traded, we were riding on the team plane together. Kevin and I used to sit next to each other on the plane on our road trips. He leaned over and said, "You know what? You see how Bennie [Blades] isn't here anymore? You see how Lomas [Brown] is not here anymore? Next year I'm not going to be here, because management doesn't want me here anymore."

I laughed. I couldn't believe it. There was no way Kevin was not going to be with the team the next year. He'd made the Pro Bowl the previous two years, and he would make it again that year. Though '97 was the year I ran for 2,000 yards, Kevin was the true leader of the team. It showed in everything he did—from the practice field, to the locker room, to the games. He was someone we couldn't replace. But Kevin insisted that management would see to it that he wasn't around, and sure enough they made the move, shipping him off to Seattle.

I didn't realize it at the time, but part of me left with him, just as part of me left with those other guys I mentioned. Football may be a violent game, but it's all about love. You have to love the game, and part of that love comes from your teammates, the guys who share the same goal of winning, the guys who create the locker room chemistry.

That dedication to winning, to doing well as part of a team of guys, is what drove me to diet, run, and lift weights during the off-season. I wanted to win—for myself and for the team. I loved the game enough to do what it takes in March and April to prepare myself to play through the following January.

During games, I put everything into it, and so the realization that some of the people you worked for weren't as committed to winning as you were slammed me harder than any linebacker had ever hit me in my entire career. That realization trivialized everything I did during the off season to prepare myself. It trivialized everything I dreamed about from the time I was a kid in Wichita, juking imaginary defenders in my front yard on North Volutsia Avenue.

As long as you know that you're headed in the right direction, that you have a fighting chance at winning, all the effort makes sense and has meaning. But by 1997, it wasn't exactly clear what they were doing, other than shipping off proven players, and replacing them with young players who were unproven.

Losing was difficult, but this really wasn't about losing. Professional football is very competitive, and you're going to lose some games. Rather, it was more about not even trying to win, and I couldn't live with that. Playing in an NFL game, at my position especially, is like surviving a major car wreck. Multiply that feeling by sixteen weeks, and you're lucky to walk away after the season. I was risking my neck, and I had

watched two of my teammates go down with spinal cord injuries, for some bean-counter who really isn't committed to winning?

As time ran out in that game against the Ravens, it also ran out in my career. I decided they could go on without me. That game, even that season, was the knockout blow, the shot that took me from inevitability to completion.

Shaking hands with lineman Kevin Glover before a game in 1997. Kevin's departure before the next season convinced me that the Lions were no longer dedicated to winning.

NOW YOU SEE HIM

Stephen Dunn/Getty Images

TIME TO MOVE ON

The season had seemed to end before it even began. We lost our first three games and seven of our first nine. After winning three in a row, we lost to San Francisco and Jacksonville back-to-back to end any outside shot at the playoffs. It was difficult to even say that we were playing for pride when we'd been out of the running for so long and were missing a half-dozen injured starters.

Except for one game in Jacksonville, I'd averaged only 3.8 yards a carry or less in the final six games of the season. Nothing was clicking. I missed my fifth consecutive 1,500-yard season by nine yards. Herman Moore missed a 1,000-yard receiving year. Robert Porcher didn't get his thirteenth sack.

"The thing that is most prevalent is disappointment," I told reporters after the Ravens game. "And really, just almost regret. It's almost like you wasted a whole year of football. That's how I feel right now."

A teammate, wide receiver Johnny Morton, said essentially the same thing: "It has been kind of emotionally draining. Like a really rough ride. I'm more drained than anything I've ever been through in my life, really. It seems like every aspect of football has been taken to the limit this year, from the mental approach to the game, to the schemes, to people trying to mesh together, everything."

I'd been through bad seasons before, but this was different. Everything around me told me that it was time to move on. I hate to use the word burnout, but that's basically what it was. As I got older, I just didn't need it. I didn't desire it. I didn't get the same charge out of playing.

I took time in the off-season to let those feeling pass, to let the frustrations subside. Bobby Ross had given me a June 1 deadline to let him know if I would be playing or not, but that deadline came and went without a word from me. He took my silence to mean that I would be returning.

Looking back, I could have done things differently, but at the time I wasn't trying to be diplomatic. I was trying to get my message out that I was finished, and I wasn't trying to make friends. I didn't do anything unethical or illegal, but you couldn't tell that from the way it was covered in the media. They were unhappy with my silence, especially after the formal announcement was released, but I didn't have anything more to say than what I'd said in my statement. There's only one thing that I would have changed: I would have wished my team good luck.

Do I regret not returning the coach's phone calls? Not really. It wasn't anything against him, but at that point nothing was going to change the circumstances, and I wasn't going to lead him on. I'd said everything I needed to say. I didn't have anything else to tell him. Maybe I should have told him that. Maybe he would have appreciated that. But for the most part, I don't regret the way I handled things.

My retirement letter didn't even hint at my frustration, because I didn't want to take shots at people as I left. I just wanted to walk away. The previous drafts of that letter, however, reeked of my general frustration. Management had let quality players slip away. We'd been losing for years. Now we were right back where we were when I

Shortly after the end of last season, I felt that
I probably would not return for the 1999-2000 season.
I also felt that I should take as much time as possible
to sort through my feelings and make sure that my feelings
were backed with conviction. Today, I officially declare
my departure from the NFL.

It was a wonderful experience to play in the NFL,
and I have no regrets. I truly will miss playing for the
Lions. I consider the Lions' players, coaches, staff,
management and fans my family. I leave on good terms
with everyone in the organization. I have enjoyed
playing for two great head coaches, Wayne Fontes and
Bobby Ross, who are good coaches and leaders. I am
not involved in a salary dispute of any kind. If I had
played this season, I would have earned a more than
satisfactory salary.

The reason I am retiring is simple: My desire to
exit the game is greater than my desire to remain in it.
I have searched my heart through and through and feel
comfortable with this decision.

I want to thank all of the fans and media who made
playing in the NFL such a wonderful experience. I have
had the pleasure of meeting many of them. Although I was
not able to honor many of your requests for autographs
and interviews, it was not because I overlooked the
importance of those who asked.

Finally, I want to thank my family and friends for
their support and guidance. I wish my teammates, coaches
and the entire Lions organization all the best.

NOW YOU SEE HIM

My retirement statement, released exclusively to the *Wichita Eagle* on July 27th of 1999.

arrived. I'd played for a period of time in which I felt I'd experienced everything in the game that I was meant to experience with that organization.

It also was the right time for me. I didn't see what good there was in hanging around when the organization wasn't trying to put together a winning team. Looking at what other teams in our division had done—teams such as Green Bay, which had brought in Reggie White, and Minnesota and Tampa Bay—I didn't think we were as serious about winning as our competitors.

PUBLIC REACTION

Though my frustration with the organization, the loss of my former teammates, and my general feeling of exhaustion all combined to fuel my decision to retire, and those seemed like clear and valid reasons, people began inventing other reasons without knowing the truth. To some people, particularly in the media, my retirement was seen as a ploy for money, as if I were only pretending to retire so that the Lions would give me a new contract. Mitch Albom of the *Detroit Free-Press* suggested as much. Most of what Mitch had said about me over the years was flattering, but some things he said after I retired were, for lack of a better word, interesting to me. I heard him talking about my retirement on the ESPN morning show "The Sports Reporters." I had always liked the commentary on the show and tried to catch it whenever possible.

During one show, they discussed my retirement, and I remember laughing and thinking to myself, "Where are these guys coming from?" Mitch made the point that

whenever you hear a guy saying that it's not about money, it's always about money. Then he referred to me. I thought, "Is this the same Mitch I've known for ten years, saying that about me? Wow." The bad part was that I thought he knew me better. Years later, he said that he felt strange as he heard himself making the statement. He realizes what he said wasn't true.

Another explanation I often heard was that I didn't care about the game. Because I don't outwardly show my feelings, some people thought I wasn't passionate about football. To prove their theory, they often pointed to the fact that I just handed the ball to the official in the end zone after I scored a touchdown. But the way I see it, my accomplishment was crossing the goal line. I didn't have to stand back and admire it. Everyone saw the play. I didn't feel the need to put it in everybody's face. I didn't mind celebrations. They just weren't me. I even appreciated the end zone celebrations of guys like Billy "White Shoes" Johnson when I was a kid. But everybody started doing it, and it got old. Before, it was just a couple of guys who did it. Now it seems like everybody has a whole choreographed little kick-ball-change thing they do.

Those things are cool, but they should never overshadow the game. It is still a team sport. Whatever you did, you had some help doing it. If I was in the Olympics running the 100 meters, that would be a whole other ballgame. But football is a team sport, and I've always thought of it that way. I felt like the weakest link should go out and practice and play as if he's just as responsible as anyone else, and that's how you win—not by pointing the finger at somebody else or trying to grab all the glory for yourself. No, I didn't dance around in the end zone after touchdowns, but I did love scoring them, and as I've said throughout this book, I love football. For most of my life it was a huge part of my life.

Yet another reason people (who don't even know me) gave for my leaving was that I wanted to leave the game before getting hurt. That's not true. I never said—or thought—that I've got to get out while I'm healthy. I think it just kind of worked out that way. I always knew there were inherent risks in the game and that I could have the same injury as anyone else who has played. But because I was a running back, I could only deteriorate so much before I couldn't play anyway. If I was hurting or deteriorating, they would have to get someone else in my position. At the same time, I'm the type of person who feels that if I'm too banged up or if the game is causing too much pain and suffering on a daily basis, I won't continue.

But I've learned through the years that you have to let people say what they want and do your best to figure out the truth for yourself. When I announced my retirement, some people didn't even try to find a reason. They were just angry. I mostly was criticized for not holding a press conference and for retiring by fax. Some letters were less than complimentary.

A guy named Jeff Primmer from Des Moines wrote: "I have been a Detroit Lions (and subsequently, a Barry) fan for more than 40 years. How can Mr. Sanders claim the Lions teammates and coaches had been like a family to him? Who would do such a thing to his family?. . . I don't begrudge Mr. Sanders his personal life. I do take particular exception to the callous, selfish, backstabbing way he treated his 'friends' and 'family.' I'd hate to experience his attitude toward those he doesn't like."

On the other hand, some people rose to my defense. George Pearson of Wichita wrote: "I have come to believe that Mr. Sanders is a man of unusual character. Many athletes are addicted to the adulation of their fans. In turn, fans come to feel that they own a piece of that athlete. It is a dependency relationship that Sanders is having no part of.... To quote a speaker that I heard recently, 'Honor is a gift that a man can only give to himself, and no other man can take it away.' That speaker could have been talking about Barry Sanders."

NO REGRETS

People ask me if I regret leaving, and the answer is no. For a while, I regretted that the Lions—after forcing me to return a $7-million signing bonus—still retained my rights. It would have been nice to play in a Super Bowl. Had we kept some of the players we traded away, we might have gotten there, and I would have liked to get there with those guys, as a Lion.

The man with whom I had the most trouble was Chuck Schmidt. He was basically a business man who came from a very traditional background. He had his favorites who he'd pay and others who he didn't want to pay. He is no longer part of the organization. All in all, I'm not the least bit bitter about my career and feel only good things about the Lions. I wish the team well, and

BARRY SANDERS

I'm looking forward to attending my first Lions game since I retired.

Part of me wants to believe that my leaving helped the organization, forced them to go in a different direction. As long as I was there, I'd fill most of the seats and sell a lot of jerseys, even during terrible seasons. From a business standpoint, there was no reason to make a change. But with me gone, they were forced to regroup, and look at what they've done recently. They've brought in a proven winner in Coach Steve Mariucci and exciting young players, such as Joey Harrington and Charles Rogers. I'm looking forward to becoming more active with the organization in whatever capacity they allow and also with the city of Detroit.

I enjoy success in my own way, and even though we never got to the Super Bowl, I enjoyed playing. As for the question of making a comeback, I don't know. Though I could very well not play anymore, I also could possibly wake up one day and say that, given the right set of circumstances, I could get back out there and play. I still watch football. College, pro, whatever. I like watching a good game. But I achieved great success as a player because I always wanted to see what I could do next, and right now

I'm interested in what I can do as a man, as a father, as a businessman, and as a golfer. While I was with the Lions, I pretty much did everything that was physically possible. I don't know what else I could have done.

My father says that I have no idea what kind of genuine joy I brought to people who watched me. I'd always told myself

NOW YOU SEE HIM

Sitting in the end zone after one of my last games, against the San Francisco 49ers.

that football was just a game, that it really didn't matter in the grand scheme of things, but it had become more than a game in my life. True, it had helped me do wonderful things for myself and my family and my community, but it had become more than a game, and that was a problem. As I said, I'd been running on fumes for years. Those feelings had overtaken me the way night falls. It is hard to attach a time to the actual sunset, but there's no mistaking when all the light is gone.

Career Stats

		RUSHING					RECEIVING			
Year	G	Att	Yards	Y/A	TD		Rec	Yards	Y/R	TD
1989	15	280	1470	5.2	14		24	282	11.8	0
1990	16	255	1304	5.1	13		36	480	13.3	3
1991	15	342	1548	4.5	16		41	307	7.5	1
1992	16	312	1352	4.3	9		29	225	7.8	1
1993	11	243	1115	4.6	3		36	205	5.7	0
1994	16	331	1883	5.7	7		44	283	6.4	1
1995	16	314	1500	4.8	11		48	398	8.3	1
1996	16	307	1553	5.1	11		24	147	6.1	0
1997	16	335	2053	6.1	11		33	305	9.2	3
1998	16	343	1491	4.3	4		37	289	7.8	0
TOTAL	**153**	**3062**	**15269**	**5.0**	**99**		**352**	**2921**	**8.3**	**10**

16

MY SPIRITUAL
W A L K

Most of my life has revolved around Sundays. As a player in the NFL, I made my living on Sunday afternoons. As a child, I learned about eternal life at church on Sundays. Back then, it sometimes felt as if I had spent an eternity in church, felt like I was born there. The spiritual beliefs I learned through the church remain a large part of my life.

Mother got us up early on those mornings, scrubbing us and dressing us for Sunday school. After Sunday school, we went to church for services. After a break, we returned to the church for an evening service. At various times, we sang in the choir, served on the usher board, and attended a mid-week service.

During the summer, Mother organized a Vacation Bible School for us and all of our friends. She still runs a Bible school today. Mother was the main force that shaped my faith, and I was lucky to have her. She influenced me perhaps more than my time in church. I had such a good example at home of what a Christian should be, and I saw that example everyday.

Our church, Paradise Baptist, was led by a wonderful minister, Reverend Paul Gray. I had a lot of respect and admiration for Reverend Gray, and I remember wanting to grow up to be a preacher. We'd even hold pretend services in our living room with me as preacher and my sisters as the choir and congregation. I don't quite remember what I said, but I remember trying to mimic the flashy ministers I had seen preaching, charismatic men with stylish suits and white leather shoes.

I loved the way they dressed and the way they held everyone's attention. Reverend Gray was not that type, but I found him interesting. I didn't always appreciate all that time in the pews, however, which I guess is pretty normal for a kid. Sometimes, sitting through those long services was as much about survival as it was about revival.

But as a young man, I found a measure of sanctuary and comfort in my faith, a sound-proof bunker where I could retreat from pressures. It gave me a way of looking at things and handling them. As I've grown older, I've come to realize that it's more important what you do when you're not in church, but the message of the church is still very valuable to me. When I was playing football, that message insulated me from much of the madness that surrounds a professional athlete. It kept me grounded.

Life as a professional athlete means a daily assault on your character. You're constantly being tested. At every strata of society, there's a desire for more money, more fame, more status. It is not difficult to find yourself becoming the perception others have of you. All of the temptations you can imagine swirl around you every day in that world. The principles of my faith helped me survive in that world before I was prepared for it. I had a certain amount of grounding that helped me remember who I was raised to be and who I should try to be. I felt fortunate to be in the NFL and enjoying a lot of success, and I tried to be thankful for those blessings.

However, I never wanted to set myself up as the moral conscience for the sports world, but that role eventually became my identity, particularly in the media. It seemed more important to people that I be the person they needed me to be— the refreshing alternative to the modern, narcissistic athlete—than to be myself, an imperfect human being with flaws just like everyone else. One situation that made news was the birth of my first child. I had just finished making an abstinence video for teenagers with pro basketball star A.C. Greene when news surfaced that I had a son but not a wife. My son, B.J. Sanders, arrived in 1994.

His mother and I dated in college, lost touch, and then we began seeing each other again. As I said, I had talked about no sex before marriage and had a certain image with the public, and I didn't hold a press conference to say that I had crossed

Above: **Family and friends gather after church** *(l-r)* **Eloise (neighbor), Robert and Cassandra Earl (neighbors), Byron, my sister Elaine, Mrs. Barry (neighbor) and my sister Krista stand behind me.** *Right:* **My son B.J., a very important part of my life, poses in his Little League uniform.** *Page 127:* **I talk to my mother, who provided a great example of a spiritual life.**

NOW YOU SEE HIM

that line. I didn't make a practice of calling press conferences.

It may sound strange, but I don't regret anything. I love being B.J.'s dad. Although it wasn't an ideal situation or the way it was supposed to be, I knew I was taking on the biggest responsibility and the biggest privilege of my life. I had wanted to be a dad, because I came from such a big family. Family was important to me. I was shocked by the news, but I was happy about it, too. It would have been great to have been married when he was born, but when I look back I wouldn't change a thing.

I think my parents were surprised when they heard about the situation, but they handled it well. They were very supportive.

After that, the most compelling emotion I felt was the desire to be a good parent. Since the beginning, I've searched for ways to be the best possible parent. I've gotten wiser, and I'm still trying to be a better person. I hope that my effort and wisdom will be reflected in the lives of my children and grandchildren.

There were and are times when holding to the spiritual path that had been lit for me was difficult, and my spiritual obligations began to feel heavy. My solid family upbringing, values, and principles—learned at church and at home—have guided and supported me. I'd hate to see how my life would have looked without that grace and guidance.

17

LIFE PLANS

I heard an older and wiser NFL retiree, former Minnesota Viking great and current state Supreme Court justice Alan Page, describe a football career as a suspension in time. Not a suspension of real time, but a suspension of a life time. Your life is, in a way, on hold.

Professional sports careers demand preparatory fidelity. As your career moves from the improbable in Little League to the possible in college, success demands intense work and focus—not simply long hours in the weight room, but on the track and on the stadium stairs. It also requires attention to flexibility and diet. You have to learn the game on a different level, as a student, too. You need to learn to read defenses not only for when you take the ball and run headlong into them, but so that you will be better able to recognize a blitz and have to put your helmet in the chest of a charging linebacker or safety to protect your quarterback.

BARRY SANDERS

Previous page: **Holding my son Nigel not long after his birth. I never get tired of watching him.** *Above:* **B.J., my friend Mick Thompson, and I take in an OSU basketball game.** *Left:* **In October of 2003, I was inducted into the College Football Hall of Fame at an OSU-Kansas State game. Pistol Pete, the OSU mascot, gives me the thumbs up.**

It is year-round work. You need to stay fit at the minimum during the off season, but many players try to gain ground or sustain high performance through a lung-busting program. Walter Payton and Jerry Rice had legendary programs, in which they sprinted through deep sand or ran several hundred yards uphill over rough and winding terrain. Those workouts contributed not only to their unbelievable on-field achievements, but also to their longevity and dearth of injury. They managed to forge bodies that were gridiron tough through their workouts.

Over time, I noticed changes in my own health habits, especially with my diet. As the healthcare industry issued many warnings about sugar and fat consumption, I could have been their poster boy. As I mentioned already, early in my career, the night before a game, you'd find me heading to my hotel room with a brown grocery sack full of all manner of sweets and confections, including my Suzy Q's. I didn't know at the time how this diet impacted my weight.

More than halfway through my career, I knew I needed to make some changes in order to boost my performance. I'd been putting up good numbers every year, but I took a lot of playful ribbing, particularly from Herman Moore, our All-Pro wide receiver, for getting caught from behind by defenders on some of my longer runs. I knew I wasn't the best I could be, and there was room for improvement.

I noticed some other aspects of form and function that I hoped to improve, particularly my knee lift and my heel turnover. While watching game film, I noticed that when I was in full stride, my knees didn't

piston very high. It didn't need to be as high as San Francisco 49er's great Roger Craig's chest-high lift, but I certainly had room to improve. I also noticed that my turnover—how close my heels came to my butt while in stride—wasn't very good either.

These inefficiencies probably robbed me of some speed and some performance. To push myself, to stretch my boundaries, (and also to properly finish off those long runs) I had to make some changes. I started with my diet. I traded in my Suzy Q's and sack-loads of candy for platefuls of fresh vegetables and more salads with less dressing. I also started a stretching regimen to increase my flexibility and improve my form. Compare game film from early in my career to later footage, and you see a slimmer me with higher knee lift and more efficient turnover. You see that I'm finishing runs on my feet in the end zone as opposed to being dragged down from behind.

I always put everything into my preparation and was pleased to see it pay off on the field. I worked hard during the season as well as during the off season to meet all of the physical challenges of facing stubborn defenses dug in to stop me. I saw the benefits of such hard work in the various successes I had on the field, but over time, I felt the routine draining me in the same way that a bad relationship can be draining. It wasn't simply the workouts (I've always loved physical activity) but a little bit of everything. I was putting far more into my career physically and emotionally than I was receiving professionally.

That's when I started thinking about what Alan Page had said about a pro career

BARRY SANDERS

representing a suspension in time. Living in this way can distort your view of what constitutes a responsible adult life. You can decide to grow up, or you can remain dependent on the system to take care of you. You have that choice. The price of that choice, however, is allowing your life to be structured and controlled by other people.

So I left on my own terms, and I'm living on my own terms. Some players see the final year of their careers as an ending, and in some cases careers end before the person is ready to move on. In my case, it ended when I was ready. I felt it was a beginning, opening up many more possibilities for my life, and I felt confident about what lay ahead.

THE ROAD AHEAD

Since retiring from the game, I have been doing some of the things everyone else does, such as investing in business, trying to better manage my earnings, caring for my parents, getting married, and raising kids. I'm involved in developing the American State Bank in Oklahoma, which keeps me busy. I'm also doing some of the things most people don't get a chance to do, such as travel when and where I want and play all the holes of golf I want.

Golf has been a special retirement boon, and I've been playing in celebrity tournaments, such as Tiger Jam. I'm also doing some of the things I should do. I participate in a number of charities, and I often look for ways to help people help themselves. I like to think that I'm good at balancing things and excelling at more than one thing at a time. I'm certainly trying to do that.

I've been married to my wife, the former Lauren Campbell of television news fame, for three years. When we met, Lauren was the weekend anchor on the NBC affiliate in Detroit. Marriage and family have been good for me. We have a son, Nigel, and are expecting another boy in February. I'm feeling about as settled as I've ever felt in my life. I'm really getting a chance to appreciate family life and raising kids. I'm enjoying the little things, such as seeing the excitement in Nigel's eyes as he swings gently in a swing at the park, sits squealing in a man-made lake of toys, or shushes me while he's watching "Dora the Explorer" on television.

I catch myself staring at him sometimes as he gets lost in what he's doing, his chubby little face a picture of concentration. I'm now lost in being a parent. We still make our home in Michigan for the time being. My goal is to create the best home that I can for them, an environment that gives them the chance to be good people, much like the one I had way back on North Volutsia Avenue in Wichita.

NOW YOU SEE HIM

Posing for a family photo with Lauren and Nigel. *Next Page:* **A family photo album.**

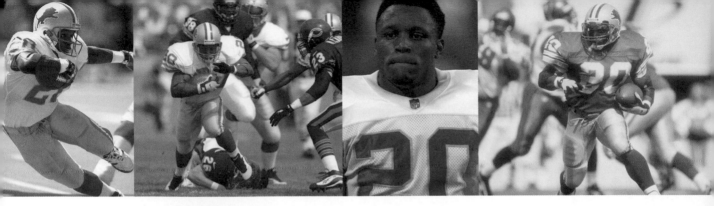

APPENDIX Pro Career / Year *by* Year

1989
Gained 1,470 yards to set the team's single-season rushing mark and the NFL rookie mark, both previously held by Billy Sims / Scored 14 rushing touchdowns, establishing a new Detroit Lions' record / Returned five kickoffs for 118 yards (23.6 avg.) / Named first-team All-Pro by Associated Press, *College & Pro Football News Weekly*, Pro Football Writers of America, *Football Digest, The Sporting News* and *Pro Football Weekly* / Voted NFL Rookie of the Year by *Sports Illustrated, The Sporting News,* NFL Films, and Pro Football Writers of America / Voted NFL Offensive Rookie of the Year by *Pro Football Weekly, Football Digest, College & Pro Football News Weekly* and Associated Press / Selected first-team All-NFC by *Football News* and United Press International / NFC Rookie of the Year by UPI / Lions' Offensive MVP and the Lions' Quarterback Club Offensive MVP / Elected to the Pro Bowl

1990
Won the NFL rushing title with 1,304 yards on 255 carries (5.1 yards-per-carry average), making him the first Detroit Lion to win that title since Byron "Whizzer" White led the league in 1940 / Scored 13 rushing touchdowns, 16 in all, tying the Lions record. Named All-Pro by AP, UPI, PFWA, *Pro Football Weekly, The Sporting News, College & Pro Football News Weekly, Sports Illustrated*'s Dr. "Z" Team, and Football News / Earned his second appearance in the Pro Bowl / Named the Lions' Offensive MVP and, with 96 points, became the first non-kicker to lead Detroit in scoring since Mel Farr and Bill Gambrell each tallied 42 points in 1968

1991
Finished second in the league in rushing (to Emmitt Smith of the Dallas Cowboys) with 1,548 yards, setting a Lions team record / Led the league in touchdowns with 17 / Named the NFL Players Association NFC Most Valuable Player / Selected *Football Digest*'s NFL Player of the Year / Won the Maxwell Football Club's Pro Player of the Year Award / Won consensus All-Pro honors (AP, UPI, PFWA, *Pro Football Weekly, The Sporting News, College & Pro Football News Weekly, Football Digest, Sports Illustrated, and Football News*) / Made third consecutive start in the Pro Bowl / Named the NFC's Offensive Player of the Month for September / Led Detroit in scoring for the second straight year / Became the first non-kicker in team history to score more than 100 points in a season (102)

1992
Finished second in the NFC and fourth in the NFL with 1,352 yards rushing / Started his fourth consecutive Pro Bowl / Earned All-NFC honors from UPI, *Football News* and *Pro Football Weekly* / Named second-team All-Pro by Associated Press, N.E.A. and *College & Pro Football News Weekly* / Went over the 5,000-yard mark for his career with 94 rushing yards in 24 carries at Pittsburgh / Became the Lions all-time rushing leader after gaining 151 yards at Cincinnati

1993
Missed the final five games of the season with a sprained knee, returning for the Wild-Card game against Green Bay to gain 169 yards on 27 carries / Before the injury, suffered against the Chicago Bears on Thanksgiving Day, led league in rushing with 1,052 yards / Had only missed two previous games in his career / Selected to start his fifth straight Pro Bowl but did not play due to injury / Surpassed the 6,000-yard rushing mark for his career when he gained 90 yards against Phoenix / Ran for what was then the second-highest rushing total of his career with 187 yards in 29 carries vs. Tampa Bay, earning NFL Player of the Week by the Pro Football Writer's of America and NFC Offensive Player of the Week / Surpassed the 1,000-yard mark for the fifth time in as many seasons with 75 yards on 17 carries at Green Bay

1994
Named NFL Player of the Year by *Football Digest* / Chosen first-team All-Pro by *The Sporting News, USA Today, College & Pro Football News Weekly, Football Digest, Pro Football Weekly,* Pro Football Writers of America and *Sports Illustrated* / Named Associated Press Offensive Player of the Year / Set a then-career-high rushing total with 1,883 yards, the sixth-highest single-season rushing total in NFL history / Set a Lions' single-game record and a career high with 237 yards against Tampa Bay / Started his sixth consecutive Pro Bowl / All-NFC first-team pick by *Football News* and United Press International / Named NFL Players Association NFC Most Valuable Player / Won the 1994 ESPN "Espy" Award for NFL Performer of the Year / Voted NFC Player-of-the-Month for October, NFC Offensive Player of the Week (Weeks 3, 10 and 16) / Surpassed the 7,000-yard mark for career with 194 yards in a career-high 40 carries at Dallas (his 40 carries are the most ever against the Cowboys) / Made the longest run of his career at Tampa Bay, an 85-yarder, after losing his shoe on the play / Made an 84-yard run against Chicago, the longest in Silverdome history and the second-longest of his career / Surpassed the 10,000-yard mark in career total yardage against the Packers / Limited to only 52 yards against Miami on Christmas Day, falling short in the quest for 2,000 yards / Led team with seven catches for 58 yards against the Dolphins / Held to minus one yard rushing, a career-low, on 13 carries and caught three passes for four yards in the Wild-Card game at Green Bay

NOW YOU SEE HIM

Named to NFC's starting Pro Bowl squad for the seventh consecutive season / Rushed for 1,500 yards / Finished with a career-high 48 receptions for 398 yards and one touchdown / Named first-team All-Pro by Associated Press, *College & Pro Football News Weekly, Football Digest, Pro Football Weekly,* Pro Football Writers of America, *The Sporting News* and *Sports Illustrated* / Was named All-NFC first-team by *Football News* and United Press International / All-Madden Team member and NFC Offensive Player of the Week for game vs. Green Bay (10/15) / Tied career-high with nine

1995 receptions (for 60 yards) against Minnesota / The streak of 803 consecutive attempts (703 rushes and 100 receptions) without a turnover was broken in the fourth quarter against Arizona / Made the longest scoring run of his career at the time, 75 yards, against Cleveland / Rushed for a season-high 167 yards on 22 carries against Green Bay / Scored two touchdowns and rushed for 120 yards against Chicago, surpassing the 1,000-yard mark for the season, becoming one of only two backs (Eric Dickerson is the other) in NFL history to rush for over 1,000 yards in each of their first seven seasons / Rushed for 54 yards at Houston (12/10), putting him over the 10,000-yard mark for his career (10th player in NFL history) / Had 10 carries for 40 yards and caught two passes for 19 yards in Wild Card game against Philadelphia

Won third NFL rushing title in dramatic fashion, gaining 175 yards at San Francisco in the final game of the season, totaling 1,553 yards, then the second-highest season total in his career / Eighth

1996 consecutive 1,000-yard season broke NFL record previously held with Eric Dickerson / Became the first player in NFL history to rush for 1,500 yards in three consecutive years / Selected as a starter in Pro Bowl for eighth straight year / Selected All Pro by *Pro Football Weekly,* Pro Football Writers of America and *The Sporting News* / Named second-team All-Pro by *College & Pro Football News Weekly*, UPI, Associated Press, and *Football Digest*

Named NFL MVP by Pro Football Writers of America, *The Sporting News, Pro Football Weekly, Football Digest, Sports Illustrated* and the Maxwell Club / Named Miller Lite Player of the Year / Named co-MVP by Associated Press / Named NFL Offensive Player of the Year by Associated Press and *College & Pro Football News Weekly* / Became only the third player in NFL history to rush for

1997 more than 2,000 yards in a season (2,053 yards), joining Eric Dickerson (2,105 in 1984) and O.J. Simpson (2,003 in 1973) / Moved into second-place on NFL's all-time rushing list with 13,778 yards, trailing only Walter Payton / Set an NFL record for most 100-yard games in a season with 14 (also a record for consecutive 100-yard games) / Recorded 100-plus yards in all eight road games, giving him an NFL record 10 such consecutive outings (dating back to 1996) / Formed with wide receiver Herman Moore the first duo from the same team since 1954 to either win or share

(Moore tied with Oakland's Tim Brown) league rushing and receiving titles in the same season / Surpassed the 1,500-yard mark for the fifth time, establishing a league record that he had shared with Walter Payton and Eric Dickerson / Became the first player in NFL history to post two 80-yard touchdown runs in one game (80 and 82 yards against Tampa Bay) and three 80-yard touchdown runs in a single season (an 80-yarder against Indianapolis) / Selected first-team All-Pro by Associated Press,

1997
Sports Illustrated, Pro Football Weekly, College & Pro Football News Weekly, The Sporting News, Football Digest and USA Today / Earned NFC Offensive Player of the Month award for October, November, and December, becoming the first NFL player to capture the award in consecutive months since Steve Young in November and December of 1994, and first ever to win the award three times in a single season / After being held to 53 yards in 25 carries in the season's first two games, he reached 100 yards in every remaining regular season game / Recorded second career 100-yard receiving game vs. Tampa Bay (9/7) with season-high eight catches for 102 yards / Held to 65 yards on 18 carries in Wild Card playoff game at Tampa Bay

Rushed for 1,491 yards and four touchdowns in team-record 343 carries in 1998 en route to tenth straight Pro Bowl selection / His 343 attempts on the year broke his own team record (342 carries in 1991) / Fell nine yards short of becoming the first player in NFL history to rush for 1,500 yards in five consecutive seasons (already the only player in history with five overall) / Named second-team All-Pro by the Associated Press / Rushed for 100 yards in five consecutive weeks, the second-longest streak of 100-yard games in his career / Two all-time NFL streaks halted in season opener at Green Bay—

1998
most consecutive 100-yard rushing games (14) and most consecutive 100-yard rushing games on the road (10) / Rushed for 155 yards against Green Bay, including a 73-yarder for a touchdown, representing the 25th time exceeded 150 yards and the 15th time scored a touchdown with a run exceeding 50 yards, and both are NFL records / Gained 140 yards against Philadelphia to surpass 1,000 yards for the season, the 10th time in his career, which tied the record held by Walter Payton / Became the second player in NFL history to exceed 15,000 rushing yards and the third player to go over the 18,000 total yardage mark / Moved into second-place on the NFL all-time total yardage list, passing Herschel Walker